Eucharistic Contemplation

Ernest Ranly, C.PP.S.

THE LITURGICAL PRESS
Collegeville, Minnesota

www.litpress.org

D1334306

Cover design by David Manahan, O.S.B.

1   2   3   4   5   6   7

Library of Congress Cataloging-in-Publication Data

Ranly, Ernest W.
    Eucharistic contemplation / Ernest Ranly.
      p. cm.
    ISBN 0-8146-2937-7 (alk. paper)
    1. Lord's Supper—Meditations. 2. Catholic Church—Prayer-books and devotions—English. I. Title.

BX2169 .R34 2003
242—dc21   2002030188

Contents

Introduction

These reflections on the Eucharist were, for the most part, prepared and delivered in the Parish of San Francisco de Borja, in Lima, Peru, as part of the Jubilee Celebration for the year 2000. Every Thursday the Blessed Sacrament was exposed for two hours of adoration. I had the responsibility to guide the second hour with song, prayer, and reflection.

This gave me the opportunity to develop some themes that had interested me for some time: eucharistic contemplation with emphasis on the spirituality of the precious blood of Christ.

The time of adoration is neither the time nor the place for classes in theology or for orientations and instructions in eucharistic contemplation. It is to be hoped that these reflections serve principally for moments of prayer. Nevertheless, there is a bottom line to these reflections; there is a thesis about what is contemplation and, specifically, what is eucharistic contemplation.

I present here for those faithful adorers of the Blessed Sacrament my style of reflections for moments of prayer and adoration. It is my hope that these reflections will serve those who look for new orientations in their prayers.

I do not speak of devotions. This is not a new prayer book of eucharistic devotions in the style very common for the past three or four centuries, even by luminaries such as Saint Alphonse Liguori and the Cure de Ars, Saint John Vianney. These are not prayers directed to Jesus in the sacrament of the altar, full of sentiments, feelings, petitions, thanksgiving, praise, reparation . . . .

One model which is key for me is the very style of the prayers of the Church; that is, the prayers of the Roman Missal and of the Sacramental Rites. With very few exceptions, liturgical prayers are directed to God, the Father, with a focus on our salvation through Jesus, the Christ, and always in union with the Holy Spirit. Very few liturgical prayers are oriented directly to Christ.

Here is an example of a Prayer after Communion, during the Easter Season:

> Let us pray
> Father,
> you have brought to fulfillment the work of our
>   redemption
> through the Easter mystery of Christ your Son.
> May we who faithfully proclaim his death and
>   resurrection in these sacramental signs
> experience the constant growth of your salvation
>   in our lives.

May this little work help some of the faithful to take up a prayer such as this—and the many others like it from the Missal—before the Blessed Sacrament. May they remain there, in silence, attentive to the "mystery of Christ" present "in these sacramental signs." In other words, instead of reading through devotional prayers in some manual, we can simply take the prayers from the Missal and pray in silent contemplation.

This is not a catechism. This is not a course of studies. Therefore, these reflections should not be read one after another. It is presumed that the reader is before the Tabernacle or before the Blessed Sacrament solemnly exposed. If there are some repetitions in the text it is to allow the reading of each reflection without making undue references to others.

The first reading of a reflection should be done very slowly, providing a basic understanding of the text. Then, perhaps, search out the various references to Sacred Scriptures. Next, reread and select a few key lines. Finally, let the Spirit breathe into your soul.

But most important, return to the Eucharist itself and remain there, in silence, in contemplation. Each written reflection presented here should serve for at least a half-hour of contemplation, of profound prayer.

Also, each reflection presumes a single individual is reading from this booklet and, therefore, all references are to the first person singular. "I am in the presence of God." When leading a group in eucharistic adoration, feel free to change the references to the first person plural. "We are in the presence of God."

The original of this work was published in Spanish in Lima, Peru, 2002 by Editorial San Pablo, Las Acacias, Miraflores. The present version is much more than a translation. If the faith is genuinely inculturated, no mere translation of words can catch the full spirit of the original. Therefore, at times, I have taken the liberty to rewrite some parts in order to address more directly a non-Peruvian public.

For example, only Mexicans can genuinely sense the mystique of Our Lady of Guadalupe. Likewise, no one outside of the Peruvian religious culture can feel the same sentiments toward Our Lord of Miracles.

Yet our common faith in the Eucharist has a universality that is not reducible to a specific culture.

It is here that eucharistic contemplation has its beginning and its end.

CHAPTER ONE

The Mystery of the Love of God

I am in the presence of God.

I am in the presence of the mystery of the love of God.

In the dialogue with Nicodemus in the Gospel of Saint John, Jesus says:

> For God so loved the world that he gave his only Son, so that everyone who believes in him may not perish but may have eternal life. Indeed, God did not send the Son into the world to condemn the world, but in order that the world might be saved through him. Those who believe in him are not condemned (John 3:16-18).

My existence, my life, my very being is discovered in the center of this mystery: God loves me; God has sent God's Son; God does not want to condemn the world, but rather to save it.

I live this mystery of the love of God in every moment of my existence.

The love of God is like the ocean and I am a drop within this immensity. But I am a drop of water that never loses its own identity. God knows and loves me as an individual person.

In a Chinese tale the little fishes of the sea, swimming in the depths of the ocean, speak up and ask of their elders: Where is the water?

The drops of water in the ocean do not live separated, isolated, independently from the water of the sea; rather, every drop is completely integrated totally as part of the water.

I, for all my individuality, do not live separated, isolated, independently from the love of God. Everything that I am, that I have, my dreams, my aspirations, are integrated into the mystery of the love of God.

How can I ask: Where does one discover the love of God? It is as if the small fishes in the depths of the ocean would ask: Where is the water? I am submerged in the love of God. The love of God is closer to me than the air that I breathe.

I now have the opportunity to take a few moments of silence, of reflection, of contemplation, to allow this mystery of the love of God to penetrate into my being.

It is pretentious to imagine that I merit, that I deserve, the love of God. It's not like that at all. God's love is a gift, something freely given, undeserved.

By my own initiative I can do nothing to have the love of God come to me. It is a given, a simple reality. It is a fact. Like the air I breathe, like the light of day.

Every day, early morning, the sun rises. The birds sing. The fields blossom. The animals leap for joy in the open country. But the birds, the flowers, the animals are not the cause, the reason why the sun rises every day. There it is: the sun! And there is a party—a fiesta. There is joy, happiness, light, life, food, drink.

Every day one discovers the love of God.

When I wake up I bless the Lord. When I walk in the gardens, in the parks, I praise God. When I greet my family, my friends, I pray to the Lord.

My blessings, my praises, my prayers are not the cause of the love of God. The love of God simply is here. And so, let us have a party. There is joy, happiness, light, life, food, drink.

But there is a need that I make myself more conscious of God's love. A need to make me more sensitive, more open, more ready to sense, to see, to recognize the love of God in my daily experiences.

Christian contemplation is the open attitude of a believer before the love of God. It is the posture of the birds before the rising of the sun. Contemplation is a direct, spontaneous reaction, a simple knowing, a simple recognition of happiness, of the reception of the love of God.

I am in the presence of God.

I am in the presence of the mystery of the love of God.

I am in the presence of the Blessed Sacrament.

Before the Sacred Host, the sacrament of life, I feel profoundly that I am in the presence of the love of God.

The Word of God took on flesh, bone, and blood through the Holy Spirit in the womb of Mary.

Through the Holy Spirit, Christ now is bread in the Eucharist.

Here and now, before the Blessed Sacrament, I am in the presence of the mystery of the love of God.

CHAPTER TWO

Eucharistic Contemplation

It is called Holy Hour. Holy because I am in the presence of God, in the presence of the Blessed Sacrament. It is a privileged hour because it is a time of prayer.

Therefore, my thoughts and my words here, before the Blessed Sacrament, are within the context of faith. This is not the time for parish announcements, for catechism lessons, for instructions, for theology.

Holy Hour and prayer is that which follows theology. Prayer is that which stays with me after studying the catechism, after doctrine, after classes of faith.

Contemplation is not a list of petitions, of intentions, of good wishes. Contemplation is not the reading of prayers from a book, the saying of the rosary or of litanies or of novenas.

Therefore, eucharistic contemplation is not that which one finds in prayer books of devotions; that is, devotions to Jesus in the Blessed Sacrament, with so many emotions, feelings, and sentiments expressed directly to the person of Jesus.

Contemplation is the simple awareness that I am in the presence of God: that I have been saved by the Blood of Christ; that I live and move in the love of God.

The first letter of Saint John reads:

> Beloved, let us love another, because love is from God; everyone who loves is born of God and knows God. Whoever does not love does not know God, for God is love. God's love was revealed among us in this way: God sent his only Son into the world so that we might live through him. In this is love, not that we loved God but that he loved us and sent his Son to be the atoning sacrifice for our sins (1 John 4:7-10).

I open my heart to the deep meaning of these verses from Saint John.

I am before the mystery of the love of God. God's love was revealed among us in this way; God sent his only Son into the world. "In this is love, not that we love God, but that God loves us"—that God loves *me*—"and sent his Son to be the atoning sacrifice for our sins."

Before the Blessed Sacrament I remain in silence, in wonder, overwhelmed, contemplating the depth of the mystery of God's love.

For my part, there is no need for a torrent of words, of petitions, of litanies, of "devotions." Of course, I know myself to be a sinner. I feel the weight of my sins. Yet God "sent his Son to be the atoning sacrifice for our sins." I am not pardoned through my actions. Only by the Blood of Christ does God forgive me.

My response is that of silence, of love, of gratitude.

God is love. To experience love is to know God.

Holy Hour is an hour of prayer.

Let my prayer be that of eucharistic contemplation.

CHAPTER THREE

Mystery/Memorial of Christ

In the sacrament of the Eucharist there is present the whole mystery of Christ. It is actual and real.

I have before me the fact that the love of God became human flesh in Christ and that Christ becomes bread for me in the Eucharist.

The foundation and basis for this mystery is the Holy Sacrifice of the Mass. In the eucharistic liturgy of the word and in the liturgy of bread and wine there is the full realization of the eucharistic action. The Mass is the making real of the work of salvation: the death and resurrection of Christ. The Mass is the living memorial, the remembrance of what Jesus did for us and what has been transmitted to us, his people, the Church. The Mass is the extension, the prolongation of the Last Supper in our time, at a very particular place, on the altar of our church.

Now, during this Holy Hour, the Blessed Sacrament is exposed upon the altar, here, today, at this time. This

Holy Hour has meaning only as the extension, the prolongation of the Holy Mass. The Sacred Host is the unleavened bread that has been consecrated in the Mass. It is the Bread of Life that has me remember and which makes present to me the whole history of salvation.

During the night of liberation from slavery in Egypt, the Israelites prepared unleavened bread. Here the eucharistic bread has me recall that moment of salvation, the liberation of the people of Israel from Egypt.

In the desert the people of Israel ate the miraculous bread, the manna. Here, today, the eucharistic bread has me recall that particular moment of salvation when God remembered the hunger of God's people in the desert.

Several times Jesus multiplied bread in the countryside so that the multitudes that followed him could eat. The eucharistic bread has me recall Jesus, his miracles of the multiplication of bread, and the many times when he ate with friends, with sinners, and with tax collectors.

At the Last Supper Jesus took unleavened bread (according to the Jewish rite of the paschal supper) and he announced that a piece of bread was his Body. "Take and eat. This is my Body." The Blessed Sacrament exposed here today, during this Holy Hour, has me recall this action.

I am not participating in the Holy Mass at this time. This is not the eucharistic action of the Mass as such. But the Blessed Sacrament here present upon the altar necessarily has reference to all those historic moments in the history of our salvation.

We speak of eucharistic adoration. But we can also speak of eucharistic contemplation. That is to say: I am now profoundly aware of the presence of the mystery of Christ here in the Sacrament of Christ.

In my room, alone, in private, I can recall the love of God who sent his only Son to save me and to save the world. The prayer in my room is a very good prayer, a good act of thanksgiving. But before the Blessed Sacrament, here present in the eucharistic bread, bread actual and visible, there is a fullness of the presence of Christ, really present in the permanent project of saving the world.

The eucharistic bread always has reference to the history, the fact of salvation. It has reference to the love of God who so loved the world that he sent his only Son to save the world.

When I approach the Blessed Sacrament to recall this history, I remain silent. I am in admiration over the goodness of God. My attitude is one of adoration. This is the best prayer there is: my silence before this mystery.

This is called eucharistic contemplation.

That is what I do at this moment.

CHAPTER FOUR

United in Blood with One Past

Once again I find myself before the Blessed Sacrament.

God is present everywhere, at every moment. The Spirit of God is encountered within the whole of my being. Saint Augustine said: "I searched for your face, O God, in all things, in all the world. I discovered you, my God, within me, in my own soul, in my own heart."

Yes, of course, God is always discovered from within.

But at this moment, leaving behind the presence of God in all of creation, with today's beautiful sun, I come into this church carrying within my heart faith in God, faith in the Spirit. And here now, with the exposition of the Blessed Sacrament, I meet Christ present in the Eucharist. It is a moment of faith, of recognition, of praise, of thanksgiving. God is here. How beautiful!

The theme during these Holy Hours is eucharistic contemplation. Contemplation is pure awareness before the mystery of Christ. Contemplation is a simple, direct looking at Christ. Contemplation is to say to Christ, "Here I am! You are here!" "Speak, O Lord, your servant is listening."

Contemplation is pure poetry. It is mystical. Externally, contemplation seems to be only silence. And so it is. Contemplation is silence. But it is a silence bursting with the presence of God. Eucharistic contemplation is my silence before the presence of Christ in the Blessed Sacrament.

Words can become the enemy of contemplation. Words can kill contemplation. Lovers are aware of that. Lovers do not need words. A smile, a caress, a touching of hand, an embrace: this is presence without words. This is contemplation.

The students in our parish school, San Francisco de Borja, anticipating the celebration of Independence Day, prepared some posters with paintings, flags, and patriotic banners. One banner, with reference to the nation's heroes, reads: "United in Blood, with One Past."

The banner says that we are united in one past. The youth wanted to say that we are all united through the blood of the heroes of our nation. In Peru we are all united, as the title of a book by José María Arguedas states: "The Many Bloods of Peru." In the history of the United States the thirteen colonies united into one, with the slogan: "United we stand. Divided we fall." We, then, are united in one past, one common past, our one and only history.

We could say something parallel in regard to who we are as Christians. We make up one Christian family. We are all united by blood, but it is union through the Blood of Christ. We are united in one past. We have one common history, the history of our salvation in Christ.

In the last reflection it was noted that the presence of Christ in the Blessed Sacrament is always the remembrance of the mystery of our salvation in Christ.

In every Holy Hour, before the benediction of the Blessed Sacrament, a prayer is chanted, which, in fact, is the very prayer from the Solemnity of the Body and Blood of Christ. This is one of the few prayers that is addressed directly to Jesus, Our Lord.

> Let us pray:
> Lord, Jesus Christ,
> you gave us the Eucharist
> as the memorial of your suffering and death.
> May our worship in this sacrament of your body and
>   blood
> help us to experience the salvation you won for us
> and the peace of your kingdom
> where you live with the Father and the Holy Spirit
> one God, for ever and ever.

The prayer points out that the sacred mysteries of the Body and Blood of Christ are intimately integrated into the mystery of the passion of Christ. We are one people, united in blood, with one past.

Eucharistic contemplation always has reference to our one and only past, to the one and only Blood, to the history of our salvation through the Blood of Christ.

"Help us to experience the salvation you won for us and the peace of your kingdom."

CHAPTER FIVE

The Blood of Christ

> Praise and thanksgiving be evermore to Jesus,
> Who with his Blood has saved us!
> Glory to the Blood of Jesus.
> Now and forever.

My thoughts bring me here to the presence of Christ in the Blessed Sacrament. Here I sense the love of God for me, a God incarnate, a God become human like me, like me in all things but sin. Christ, born of the Holy Spirit, died for me. His resurrection gives me the assurance of eternal life. In the Eucharist I am always in the presence of the whole mystery of Christ, the sacrament of my salvation.

Furthermore, I want to arrive at eucharistic contemplation from the perspective of the Blood of Christ.

Many times in our prayers to the Precious Blood we repeat these lines:

Praise and thanksgiving be evermore to Jesus,
Who with his Blood has saved us!
Glory to the Blood of Jesus.
Now and forever.

Before the mystery of Christ I am conscious that I have been redeemed by the precious blood of Christ. I praise and give thanks to Jesus present in the Blessed Sacrament with the knowledge and the profession of faith that Jesus has redeemed me with his Blood.

The whole Christ is permanently present in the Blessed Sacrament in the form of consecrated bread, the Sacred Host. Christ is present in the fullness of his being, as God and as human, in his divinity and in his humanity. Christ is present in that humanity glorified in the Resurrection. Therefore, when I take Holy Communion, even if I receive only the Sacred Host, I receive the fullness of Christ's Body and Blood.

In a parallel manner, my contemplation of Christ in the Blessed Sacrament is to the one, whole Christ. Therefore, eucharistic contemplation is the contemplation of the Blood of Christ, that one Christ "who with his Blood has saved us."

I am a sinner. I am a child of Adam and Eve. Even though I am created according to the image and likeness of God, I, who am of the human family, am of a perverse race. I am one of the lost sheep. I feel the reality of sin in the world of today: wars, violence of all types, robberies, injustices, corruption, violations, divorces, abortions. In my personal life, in my family there are so many arguments, bad intentions, suspicions. Sins beyond numbering.

"Who with his Blood has saved us."

God does not abandon God's people. The mystery of Christ is the mystery of that love of God who so loved us that he sent us his only Son. The Son of God came to save the world and to save me by the shedding of his Blood.

In his letter to the Romans, Saint Paul writes:

> For while we were still weak, at the right time Christ died for the ungodly. Indeed, rarely will anyone die for a righteous person—though perhaps for a good person someone might actually dare to die. But God proves his love for us in that while we still were sinners Christ died for us. Much more surely then, now that we have been justified by his blood, will we be saved through him from the wrath of God. For if while we were enemies, we were reconciled to God through the death of his Son, much more surely, having been reconciled, will we be saved by his life. But more than that, we even boast in God through our Lord Jesus Christ, through whom we have now received reconciliation (Rom 5:6-11).

"Who with his Blood has saved us."

The moment of eucharistic contemplation is a moment of reflection over my condition as a sinner. It is a moment of remorse. But much more, it is a moment of praise and thanksgiving to Christ who saves me with his Blood.

"Praise and thanksgiving be evermore to Jesus."

This is not exactly the moment for an examination of conscience. There is another time for that, such as preparing for the sacrament of reconciliation. But, of course, YES, I am conscious that I am a sinner: a sinner contrite and pardoned. A sinner redeemed by the Blood of Christ.

Therefore, before the Blessed Sacrament, humbly but joyfully, I say:

> Praise and thanksgiving be evermore to Jesus,
> Who with his Blood has saved us!
> Glory to the Blood of Jesus.
> Now and forever!

CHAPTER SIX

The Seven Offerings of the Blood of Christ

Eternal Father,
we offer you the Precious Blood of Jesus,
poured out on the cross
and offered daily on the altar.

Again I find myself before the Blessed Sacrament with a deep sense of adoration.

Christ is present, here, now, in the sacrament. Christ is present in the fullness of the mystery of salvation. In the sacred monstrance there is the consecrated bread, containing the whole history of our salvation, from the liberation of the people of Israel, the miraculous bread—manna—in the desert, the Last Supper, and, above all, the death and the resurrection of Jesus. Christ is present in a memorial of our redemption, a memorial, active, actual, living.

In the tradition of the Religious Congregation of the Precious Blood there is a prayer called "The Seven Offerings of the Precious Blood." For more than 150 years this prayer has been part of the tradition of the sisters and missionaries of the Precious Blood.

The number seven, of course, is a sacred number in all of Sacred Scripture and in the Christian/Catholic tradition. In the case of the Seven Offerings there is reference to the seven blood sheddings of Christ:

1. the circumcision,
2. the agony in the garden,
3. the scourging at the pillar,
4. the crowning with thorns,
5. the carrying of the cross,
6. the crucifixion on Calvary,
7. the piercing of the side.

There is also another devotion to the Blood of Christ called the Chaplet of the Precious Blood that has seven reflections and prayers upon these seven individual blood sheddings.

The prayer of the Seven Offerings has seven distinct intentions or petitions. These petitions correspond very well with the order and the style of the Universal Prayer prayed by the priest and the people in the liturgy of the Mass. But the tradition and wording of the Seven Offerings antedates Vatican II by more than a century.

In the Seven Offerings the opening refrain is repeated in the style of a litany. It is to be noted that, similar to the prayers in the Missal, the "offering" of the redeeming Blood of Christ is made to the Father.

Jesus, who perfectly complies with the will of his Father, says: "Father, into your hands I commend my spirit" (Luke 23:46).

Thus we see that the prayer explicitly makes reference to the historical death of Christ on the Cross. The manner of his death is that of a sacrifice, a sacrifice of blood, the precious blood of Christ to God the Father.

The title "Eternal Father," "Eternal God" is a title of highest respect, a title to an almighty God, a provident God, always present in all places and for all ages.

Although God is addressed as "eternal," this is not a distant, abstract God. It is God who is Father, Abba-Father. We address God intimately. This is very clear in Spanish where we speak to God as "You" and not as "Thou." "We offer you, my dear God, Abba, my dear Daddy, Papá, Papá God."

So we have two aspects. A God eternal and almighty. Yet a God intimate, close, my dear Daddy God.

> Eternal Father
> we offer you the Precious Blood of Jesus,
> poured out on the cross.

I am not a passive spectator at the crucifixion. Rather, like the priests of the Old Testament, I (we) "offer" the blood of the sacrificial victim to God. It is as if I am at the moment of sacrifice and I am an active participant in the offering of the Blood of Christ to God the Father.

On the other hand, the prayer of the Seven Offerings does not only make reference to the historical past, that which occurred only once on Calvary almost

2000 years ago. Rather, this same Blood is offered today by the Holy Spirit "daily on the altar." Thus we have a direct reference to the Holy Eucharist. The reference is principally to the Mass itself. But here in the Blessed Sacrament there is also present the Blood of Christ.

These lines can serve very well to be repeated when I am in silence before the Blessed Sacrament. They serve well as a model of eucharistic contemplation. These lines are an expression of my faith and my participation in the work of salvation:

> Eternal Father,
> we offer you the Precious Blood of Jesus,
> poured out on the cross
> and offered daily on the altar.

CHAPTER SEVEN

Bread as Living Remembrance

Bread is bread, made from flour, water, and salt. The flour is made from grains of wheat, ground, mixed together. Chemically, materially, bread is nothing more than bread and the eucharistic bread does not escape from the same scientific analysis.

Yet for me, a believer, the bread of the Sacred Host contains the whole remembrance of Christ: of Jesus conceived by the Holy Spirit in Mary, Jesus crucified on the cross, Jesus risen in the glory of his resurrected body. Christ, in the sacrament of the altar, mysteriously but really makes present the whole history of our salvation to me, a person of faith.

It is difficult to understand how a thing so little, such as a small piece of bread, can be a symbol of a reality so profound, a symbol of Christ and of salvation.

At this point, Father Ernest Ranly wants to share a very personal experience:

> *While still a youth of fourteen, I left my family to enter a minor seminary. This was a time of another discipline, a different style of priestly formation in the Church.*
>
> *During these years one of my older sisters was married. But, of course, I was not permitted to leave the seminary to take part in the Mass and in the family celebration.*
>
> *However, with great love, my sister saved a piece of the wedding cake. She wrapped it carefully and sent it to me by mail. My superior gave me the package that I recognized as a piece of my sister's wedding cake.*
>
> *I invited two of my best friends to share it with me. We found a secret and quiet place. We opened the package and we three ate that little piece of cake with great emotion.*
>
> *This was not like any other piece of candy or chocolate. At Christmas we all received great quantities of sweets, cookies, cakes, and there was a big exchange between all of us. We ate those Christmas goodies with great enjoyment.*
>
> *But the piece of my sister's wedding cake was something altogether different. This was not simply another piece of cake. There was a feeling, a value, something very personal and real in this piece of cake.*
>
> *It was a symbol of my sister's wedding. My companions and I came to participate in her wedding by sharing that piece of cake. The chemistry, the ingredients, its flavor—it was homemade—were not important. The full reality of that piece of cake was that it was transformed into being a symbol. It was a living remembrance of my sister's wedding.*

We have something similar in the Eucharist. Bread and wine are material things with their respective material realities. But all of this is converted into a different reality, in becoming that which Jesus did for us for our salvation.

This is not pure fantasy, a simple product of the imagination, of feelings, of memories. For example, on the day of my sister's wedding I suffered feelings of homesickness, of absence, of being distant from the family celebration. But eating that piece of wedding cake and sharing deep feelings with my buddies was a moment of living remembrance.

That is to say, to have at hand a piece of cake, to share something material, is a very special gesture and communication. It is almost a rite, poetry in action, a dramatization that touches upon reality in a most distinctive manner.

Here and now, during this Holy Hour, I have before me the eucharistic bread that brings me into a living remembrance of the person of Jesus, the memory of his work of redemption for the human family.

Yes, it is a fact that the host is bread made from grains of wheat. But the bread disappears in the eyes of faith because I perceive in the host the presence of Jesus, my Savior.

Here before the Blessed Sacrament, before this bread of living remembrance, in some way or other, I am present at the Last Supper. I am present with Mary, the Mother of Jesus, standing below the cross. I am present with Mary Magdalene embracing the feet of the "gardener" near the empty tomb of Jesus.

Eucharistic contemplation always takes into account the whole mystery of Christ.

I am taken up into this mystery.

CHAPTER EIGHT

Proclaim the Mystery of Faith

The presider—the priest (or the principal celebrant)—at the eucharistic liturgy, during those most solemn moments of the consecration, very clearly and distinctly repeats the gestures and the words of Jesus at the Last Supper. "This is my body." Then he shows the consecrated host to the people, places it on the paten, and genuflects in adoration.

He then continues and announces: "This is the cup of my blood." He shows the chalice to the people, places it on the corporal, and genuflects in adoration.

There is a tradition very popular in some parts of the world, especially in Latin America, in which all the people answer after each presentation of the eucharistic elements: "My Lord and my God."

This is a very positive tradition. It permits the assembly to participate actively at this dramatic moment of the Liturgy of the Eucharist. But since Vatican

Council II there are other instructions for this most solemn moment of the Mass.

The English version for celebrating the Mass gives the celebrant only one formula for the eucharistic acclamation: "Let us proclaim the mystery of faith." In the original Latin Missal from Rome there is only the phrase *"mysterium fidei,"* mystery of faith. The Missal in Spanish has several options, and the first and most used has two alternatives: "This is the Sacrament of our faith" or "This is the mystery of faith."

It should be very carefully noted just what is proclaimed. One does not hear, "This is the sacrament of the Eucharist" or "Here we have the Body and Blood of Christ" or "Here is the Blessed Sacrament." Rather, the celebrant sings or says, "Let us proclaim the mystery of faith." That is to say, here we have the summary, the focus, the very center of our faith, precisely here at this moment of the Eucharist.

What is the difference between "the sacrament of our faith" and "the mystery of faith"?

On one hand, this is a play of words. In Greek the word is *mysterion;* the Latin translation is *sacramentum.* In a simple linguistic case, there is no difference between mystery and sacrament.

Nevertheless, for most of us the word "sacrament" has its limitations and refers almost exclusively to the seven sacraments, within which the Eucharist is the supreme and the most perfect sacrament.

The churches of the East (the Greeks and the Russians) understand the word "mystery" as the whole mystery of Christ in his role in the salvation of the world. In this tradition, "the mystery of faith" is Christ himself, the whole history of Christ, the incarnation, birth, baptism, his miracles, his preaching, and, above all, the death and resurrection of Christ.

When the celebrant places the eucharistic elements upon the altar, he presents them to the people by singing (or saying): "Let us proclaim the mystery of faith." There is here a meaning very profound and far reaching. The acclamation by the community of believers is an echo of the fullness of our faith: "Christ has died. Christ is risen. Christ will come again."

This acclamation by the Church from the Missal is much deeper and wider than the traditional response: "My Lord and my God." "My Lord and my God" is an expression of a static faith. It says that the bread and wine have been transformed into the Body and Blood of Christ. It states that this fact is now upon the altar. The catechetical preparation for First Communion often stops at this point.

But the phrase "the mystery of faith" refers to Christ today, yesterday, and always. "The mystery of faith" is a statement of the fullness of our salvation in Christ.

"Let us proclaim the mystery of faith."

There is no better prayer, no better expression of my faith every time I come into the presence of the Blessed Sacrament.

Here today, before the exposition of the Sacred Host, I myself proclaim the mystery of faith. "Christ has died. Christ is risen. Christ will come again."

CHAPTER NINE

O Holy Banquet

> How holy this feast
> in which Christ is our food:
> his passion is recalled,
> grace fills our hearts
> and we receive a pledge of the glory to come.

This short antiphon or prayer verse, which in Latin has the name *O sacrum convivium*, was written by Saint Thomas Aquinas in the thirteenth century. Saint Thomas is not only a great Christian philosopher, but is also one of the most distinguished theologians in the whole of Christianity. He wrote (in Latin) various hymns to the Blessed Sacrament, such as *"Pange lingua,"* whose last two verses we often sing at Benediction under the title of its first two words: *"Tantum ergo."*

A sacrament is a visible sign of the invisible grace of God. A sacrament is a physical thing, a gesture, accompanied with words, which makes real a fact of salvation. For example, in baptism someone is immersed in water (or has water poured over the head) along with the saying of words and the intentions of the minister. In these actions sins are washed away and the person is born a child of God.

The gesture with water and the precise words are living remembrances of the baptism of Jesus and a remembrance of his command: "Go therefore and make disciples of all nations, baptizing them in the name of the Father and of the Son and of the Holy Spirit" (Matt 28:19). Through my own baptism I have been baptized in the death and in the resurrection of Jesus. I have been born to eternal life through the living waters of the Spirit.

And this is how it is with the sacrament of the Eucharist. Through bread—a physical thing—and through the rite of the Mass, Jesus, my life and my salvation, is made present. The invisible love of God is made visible in the bread in the mystery of faith, always most profound and mysterious.

Let us return to the short poem of Saint Thomas, *"O sacrum convivium"*:

> How holy this feast
> in which Christ is our food:
> his passion is recalled,
> grace fills our hearts
> and we receive a pledge of the glory to come.

There is reference to the fullness of human time—the past, the present, and the future:

- "his passion is recalled"—the past;
- "Christ is our food: grace fills our hearts"—the present;
- "a pledge of the glory to come"—the future.

In the same way, after the consecration of the Mass, all of us, the believing assembly, proclaim:

- "Christ has died"—the past;
- "Christ is risen"—the present;
- "Christ will come again"—the future.

The other acclamations have the same reference to time:

- "Dying you destroyed our death"—the past;
- "rising you restored our life"—the present;
- "Lord Jesus, come in glory"—the future.

- "When we eat this blood and drink this cup"—the present;
- "we proclaim your death, Lord Jesus"—the past;
- "until you come in glory"—the future.

This concept of time is an integral element in my eucharistic contemplation. Here, the eucharistic bread exposed in the monstrance is a living presence, a saving presence of Christ. "And remember, I am with you always, to the end of the age" (Matt 28:20). At the same time, as we have noted several times, the Eucharist is always a remembrance of the whole past history of salvation, above all its culmination in the passion and death of Jesus. The Blessed Sacrament here in the present celebrates the memorial of the past.

And also the Blessed Sacrament is the anticipation of the future. "We receive a pledge of the glory to come." "Christ will come again." Or, as Jesus says in the second to the last verse of the last book of the Bible, "Surely I am coming soon. Amen. Come, Lord Jesus!" (Rev 22:20). And this is what the eucharistic assembly repeats in the other proclamations after the consecration of the Mass. "Lord Jesus, come in glory!" "Lord Jesus, until you come in glory."

Let us focus a moment on the future. Before the Blessed Sacrament one may also think about the future: my future with God. The sacrament is "a pledge of the glory to come." The Eucharist is a type of guarantee, an insurance, on the part of Christ and his new and everlasting covenant with me.

I have so many worries. I am so anxious, so nervous, so occupied with economic problems, difficulties with my family, with my health. There is a danger that the little time I have before the Blessed Sacrament I fill up with prayers and petitions.

But eucharistic contemplation is something else. It is placing myself before Christ with confidence, with peace, with the experience of his past mercies, with hope for the future, to the final hope of the Second Coming of Christ.

"Your kingdom come."

"Come, Lord Jesus!"

CHAPTER TEN

Blood of the Covenant

Saint Luke gives this account of the Last Supper:

> Then he [Jesus] took a loaf of bread, and when he had given thanks, he broke it and gave it to them, saying, "This is my body, which is given for you. Do this in remembrance of me." And he did the same with the cup after supper, saying, "This cup that is poured out for you is the new covenant in my blood" (Luke 22:19-22).

The words of consecration of the Mass are a summary/composite of the three Synoptic Gospels and of Saint Paul. This is the text from the Missal for the consecration of the chalice:

> When supper was ended, he took the cup.
> Again he gave you [God the Father] thanks and praise,
> he gave the cup to his disciples, and said:
>   Take this, all of you, and drink from it:
>   this is the cup of my blood,

> the blood of the new and everlasting covenant.
> It will be shed for you and for all
> so that sins may be forgiven.
> Do this in memory of me.

Our eucharistic contemplation should also focus upon the "the blood of the covenant."

In the Gospel of Saint Luke, Jesus said: "This cup that is poured out for you is the new covenant in my blood." The words from the Missal of the Mass are: "This is the cup of my blood, the blood of the new and everlasting covenant."

A covenant is a pact, a treaty, an agreement between two persons, two parties. Other words are "alliance" or "testament." Traditionally we speak of the two Testaments in the history of salvation: the Old Testament and the New Testament. Recently it is more common to say the Old and the New Covenants. It is the same thing, only different words.

The point here is that a covenant is sealed with blood. In the Old Testament the covenant between God and God's people is sealed with the blood of animals. In the New Testament the covenant is sealed with the precious blood of Christ.

Let us turn to that dramatic moment in the history of salvation, the moment of the sealing of the first covenant between God and God's people:

> Moses came and told the people all the words of the LORD and all the ordinances; and all the people answered with one voice, and said, "All the words that the LORD has spoken we will do." And Moses wrote down all the words of the LORD. He rose early in the

morning, and built an altar at the foot of the mountain, and set up twelve pillars, corresponding to the
twelve tribes of Israel. He sent young men of the
people of Israel, who offered burnt offerings and sacrificed oxen as offerings of well-being to the LORD.
Moses took half of the blood and put it in basins, and
half of the blood he dashed against the altar. Then he
took the book of the covenant, and read it in the hearing of the people; and they said, "All that the LORD has
spoken we will do, and we will be obedient." Moses
took the blood and dashed it on the people, and said,
"See the blood of the covenant that the LORD has
made with you in accordance with all these words."
. . . And they ate and drank (Exod 24:3-8, 11).

One can make many commentaries on this passage.
On one hand, it is practically the liturgy of our Mass.
There is the assembly of the people. There is the one
who presides—Moses. There is the reading of the
Word of God. There is the response of the people in
faith and in making their commitment. There is a sacrifice of burnt offerings. There is also a sacrifice of
communion in which "all ate and drank."

And there is the ritual use of blood in sacrifice and
in the sprinkling of the people.

Now I return again here in the presence of Jesus in
the Blessed Sacrament. In the Last Supper Jesus left us
a remembrance "of the new and everlasting covenant." It was his own blood, poured out on the cross,
which brought about our redemption, which sealed the
new and everlasting covenant with God.

In whatever treaty or covenant or testament, the
document must be properly signed and sealed. With

Moses, the first covenant between God and God's people was sealed with the blood of animals. With Christ, the new and everlasting covenant is signed and sealed with his own most precious blood.

Before Christ in the Blessed Sacrament I am like Moses and like the people of Israel.

"See the blood of the covenant that the LORD has made with you."

"All that the LORD has spoken we will do, and we will be obedient."

CHAPTER ELEVEN

"Remove the sandals from your feet, for the place on which you are standing is holy ground"

The reflection today begins with a rather long reading from Exodus 3:1-6:

> Moses was keeping the flock of his father-in-law Jethro, the priest of Midian; he led his flock beyond the wilderness, and came to Horeb, the mountain of God. There the angel of the LORD appeared to him in a flame of fire out of a bush; he looked, and the bush was blazing, yet it was not consumed. Then Moses said, "I must turn aside and look at this great sight, and see why the bush is not burned up." When the LORD saw that he had turned aside to see, God called to him out of the bush, "Moses, Moses!" And he said, "Here I am." Then he said, "Come no closer! Remove the sandals from your feet, for the place on which you are

standing is holy ground." He said further, "I am the
God of your father, the God of Abraham, the God of
Isaac, and the God of Jacob." And Moses hid his face,
for he was afraid to look at God.

I am here in the presence of God, in adoration of
Christ present in the Blessed Sacrament.

In many cultures and religious traditions one must
remove all shoes to enter into a sacred place. For example, to enter a Hindu temple or an Islamic mosque
one must take off one's shoes. I should not lose this
sense of reverence, of respect, of veneration in a
Catholic church, here in my parish church. Here the
Blessed Sacrament is respectfully reserved. "The place
on which you are standing is holy ground."

"Remove the sandals from your feet!"

Later in the life of Moses and in the history of the
liberation of the Israelite people, the Lord said to Moses:

> "Come up to me on the mountain, and wait there. . . ."
> Then Moses went up on the mountain, and the
> cloud covered the mountain. The glory of the LORD
> settled on Mount Sinai, and the cloud covered it for
> six days; on the seventh day he called to Moses out of
> the cloud. Now the appearance of the glory of the
> LORD was like a devouring fire on the top of the
> mountain in the sight of the people of Israel. Moses
> entered the cloud, and went up on the mountain.
> Moses was on the mountain for forty days and forty
> nights (Exod 24:12, 15-18).

In Sacred Scripture the glory of God is presented as
a cloud. There was the belief that no one could look

upon the face of God. To look at God face to face was to die. That is why "Moses hid his face, for he was afraid to look at God."

> [In the Transfiguration,] Jesus took with him Peter and James and his brother John and led them up a high mountain, by themselves. And he was transfigured before them, and his face shone like the sun, and his clothes became dazzling white. . . . While he was still speaking, suddenly a bright cloud overshadowed them (Matt 17:1-2, 5).

Jesus here is the new Moses, who appears with Elijah in the Transfiguration. The experience of the three apostles who accompanied Jesus on the mountain is similar to those of Moses on Sinai. Also in the Ascension, as Mary and the disciples "were watching, he [Jesus] was lifted up, and a cloud took him out of their sight" (Acts 1:9).

God comes to God's people. But the divinity is hidden by a cloud that is both transparent and dark. In Jesus, the divinity is hidden in his humanity. But in the experience of the apostles in the Transfiguration and in the Ascension there is no doubt about the divinity of Jesus.

Saint Thomas Aquinas says that in the Eucharist, both the divinity and the humanity of Jesus are obscured in the eucharistic bread. The smoke of incense before the Blessed Sacrament is a gesture to symbolize that behind the cloud and smoke, that in the bread of the Host, God in Christ is present.

I must demonstrate my faith and my reverence by my silent contemplation before the Blessed Sacrament.

"Come no closer. Remove the sandals from your feet, for the place on which you are standing is holy ground."

"Moses hid his face, for he was afraid to look at God."

With Peter, I say in my heart: "Lord, it is good for me to be here."

CHAPTER TWELVE

"I Am Who I Am"

Epiphany means "manifestation." Ordinarily one thinks of Epiphany as the feast of the Three Kings, the Twelfth Day of Christmas. This is "the making manifest" of the Child Jesus as the Savior to all the peoples of the world.

But there are many "manifestations" of God in the history of Salvation. Two principal revelations of God to Moses were on Mount Sinai and in the Burning Bush on Mount Horeb. Let us return to Moses in this most extraordinary encounter with God.

This manifestation of God was not simply a personal or mystical experience for Moses himself. Rather, at this moment, God called Moses to liberate God's people from the power of the Egyptians.

"The cry of the Israelites has now come to me; I have also seen how the Egyptians oppress them. So come, I will send you to Pharaoh to bring my people, the Israelites, out of Egypt" (Exod 3:9-10).

Moses had his doubts. "Who am I that I should go to Pharaoh, and bring the Israelites out of Egypt?"

God answered Moses, "I will be with you."

But Moses insisted, "If . . . they ask me 'What is his name?'"

> [And God responded,] "I AM WHO I AM." He said further, "Thus you shall say to the Israelites, 'I AM has sent me to you.'" God also said to Moses, "Thus you shall say to the Israelites, 'The LORD, the God of your ancestors, the God of Abraham, the God of Isaac, and the God of Jacob has sent me to you.'
>
> This is my name forever,
> and this my title for all generations" (Exod 3:13-15).

Our God—my God—is a living God.

God is the God of salvation, the God of history.

Here I am with the Lord Jesus in the Eucharist. This is Christ in his fullness: incarnation, birth, his preaching the reign of God, his death and resurrection. I AM WHO I AM is the God of our ancestors in the faith: the God of Abraham, of Isaac, of Jacob. And it is the God present to me every moment of every day. I AM WHO I AM is the same Jesus, our Lord, the Christ, the one Savior, yesterday, today and forever.

I AM WHO I AM—YHWH—is a faithful God. A God who keeps his word. A God who does not abandon his people. God said to Moses: "I will be with you." Jesus said: "And, remember, I am with you always, to the end of the age."

In some prayers, such as the Seven Offerings of the Precious Blood, we call upon God with the title "Eternal Father." This, again, is to say that God is an all-faithful God, I AM WHO I AM, who fulfills his covenant with his people. Because he is God, who lives and reigns in the Unity of the Holy Spirit, forever and ever, YHWH, God, the Eternal Father.

The Lord YHWH, God, accompanies his people for all of history. In the desert, where the people of Israel were nomads. They had established no cities. They were twelve tribes, one tribe for each of the twelve sons of Jacob. They lived off the flocks of sheep and goats. Month after month they hunted for better pastureland for their animals. Therefore, they had no temple, no grotto, no fixed church.

But God stayed with the people, a pillar of smoke by day and a pillar of fire by night. They constructed the ark of the covenant (in the style of a carrying platform for statues), which they always carried with them. And the Glory of the Lord accompanied them until they came to the Promised Land.

In Canaan they built grottoes or sanctuaries where they set up the ark of the covenant. It is there that the people of Israel found a very special presence of God. Finally, Solomon constructed the Temple in Jerusalem. In the Temple there was "the Holy of Holies" where, in a very special manner, there was felt the presence of God.

In the Prologue of the Gospel of Saint John we find a figure of the Incarnation, "God-with-us": Emmanuel. "And the Word became flesh and lived among us, and we have seen his glory, the glory as of a father's only son, full of grace and truth" (John 1:14).

In the sacrament of the Eucharist I have "God-with-us," the ever-faithful God, I AM WHO I AM, the fullness of the new and eternal covenant. I have him who promised us: "And remember, I am with you always, to the end of the age."

CHAPTER THIRTEEN

The Meeting Tent

I am integrally part of a pilgrim people. I have no permanent home here on earth. I yearn for an eternal homeland. A famous prayer describes the earth as "a valley of tears." A hymn sings of "the thirst for eternity."

The people of Israel in the desert were literally, historically, a pilgrim people. They were nomads. They lived in tents, in collapsible dwellings something like the wigwams of the Native Americans on the western plains. Every day they hunted for fresh pastures for their sheep. They made temporary camp where for the moment the pastures were green.

The desert (now the translation is wilderness) is immense, empty, full of dangers and evil elements. Therefore, like the wagon trains crossing the American plains, every night the people closed the camp and put up guards like sentinels to protect the animals and to look after the security of the people in the camp.

It was in this situation that God stayed with his people, YHWH, "I AM WHO I AM," a God always faithful, a God who never abandoned his people.

In the desert God commanded Moses and Aaron to construct a very special tent outside the camp, close to the entrance to the camp. Here there was always present the Glory of God. Here God was present. In Hebrew, the presence of God is called *Shekinah*. It was a column of smoke by day and a column of fire by night.

The presence of God with the people in the Old Testament is a figure of the presence of Christ in the Blessed Sacrament. The presence of Christ is in the fullness of the mystery of faith, the fullness of the history of salvation. It is very valuable for us to accompany our ancestors in their wanderings in the desert. Because, at bottom, we are a pilgrim people.

The tent of God outside the camp has many names. On the Mount of the Transfiguration Peter said to Jesus: "Lord, it is good for us to be here; if you wish, I will make three dwellings here, one for you, one for Moses, and one for Elijah" (Matt 17:4).

Other translations of this passage say "tents" or "tabernacles." The reference is the tent at the entrance of the camp of the Israelites in the desert, where they encountered the presence of God, a God dwelling with the people.

Let us recall the dramatic ceremony of the readings of the Ten Commandments and the sealing of the first covenant between God and God's people with the blood of animals. There was a big sacrifice of animals and also a communion feast of eating and drinking.

The people replied: "All that the Lord has spoken we will do, and we will be obedient."

After that God commanded that they make "an ark of acacia wood," with many detailed directions about its construction (Exodus 25; 26; 27). Other names for this tent are the tent of encounter, the tent of presence, the tent of meeting, the tent of the covenant, the tent of testimony, the tent of revelation, the tent of dwelling (which is identical to "tabernacle"). The tent itself was like a portable sanctuary and it accompanied the Israelites for all their wanderings in the desert.

Briefly, then, this sanctuary of the desert consisted of a structure made of wood, covered and adorned with pieces of cloth and animal skins of fine quality and great elegance. Like the future temple, it was divided into two parts with a curtain separating the holy place from the most holy place.

It was called the tent of presence or the tent of dwelling because God was present in this sanctuary by means of a cloud. God had come down from the heights of Sinai to be with the people. It was called the tent of encounter, the meeting tent, the tent of revelation, because Moses and the Israelites met their God in this place and it was here that God revealed to them God's will. It was called the tent of covenant or the tent of testimony because there was preserved in the ark the two stone tablets of the Law, which was the Testament—the Constitution, the Magna Carta—of the covenant between God and the people.

Now let us read directly from the book of Exodus:

> Now Moses used to take the tent and pitch it outside
> the camp, far off from the camp; he called it the tent of
> meeting. And everyone who sought the LORD would go
> out to the tent of meeting, which was outside the camp.
> Whenever Moses went out to the tent, all the people
> would rise and stand, each of them, at the entrance of
> their tents and watch Moses until he had gone into the
> tent. When Moses entered the tent, the pillar of cloud
> would descend and stand at the entrance of the tent, and
> the LORD would speak with Moses. When all the people
> saw the pillar of cloud standing at the entrance of the
> tent, all the people would rise and bow down, all of
> them, at the entrance of their tent. Thus the LORD used
> to speak to Moses face to face, as one speaks to a friend.
> Then he would return to the camp (Exod 33:7-11).

We find in this reading many elements for reflection. God is made present in a cloud; God remains with
the people. God permits the people, especially Moses,
to speak with God, "face to face, as one speaks to a
friend." What intimacy!

All this is in anticipation of the presence of God
here, with me, in the person of Jesus, here in the
Blessed Sacrament. During his mortal life Jesus spoke
with people, such as Mary Magdalen and the beloved
disciple John, "as one speaks to a friend."

Christ has stayed with us in the Blessed Sacrament.
I can leave the "camp" of my house, the "camp" of my
work, the "camp" of my daily worries to find myself
here in this church, in this "tent of meeting." The

glory of God is present here in the exposition of the Blessed Sacrament.

I beg humbly but confidently that Jesus will speak to me "face to face, as one speaks to a friend."

CHAPTER FOURTEEN

"And he lived among us"

"And the Word became flesh and lived among us" (John 1:14).

These lines are from the prologue of the Gospel of John.

"In the beginning was the Word, and the Word was with God, and the Word was God" (John 1:1).

There are different translations, different ways to say the same thing. "He dwelt among us." "He became man," or much better, "he became human." "He took on our flesh and blood."

The point of our faith is that the Word, that is, God, became a creature with a mortal body, that the Son of God became a human being. As we say in the Divine Praises after the benediction of the Blessed Sacrament: "Blessed be Jesus, true God and true man"—truly human.

"And the Word became flesh." "He dwelt among us." "He lived among us." In a more technical biblical sense, Saint John in Greek makes reference to the Hebrew, which would say: "He put up his tent with us." "He camped with us." He made his dwelling with us, but this dwelling was a tent.

God remained with the people in the desert. The tent of meeting was always at the entrance of the camp of the Israelites. This served as a sacred sanctuary where God—faithfully present—remained at the side of his people. I AM WHO I AM.

In the prologue to John's Gospel, in order to say that the Word lived among us, as we saw, Saint John tried to say: "He put up his tent with us." "He camped with us." "He tented in our camp." God is totally inculturated into the human community.

Christ present in the Blessed Sacrament, present in the eucharistic bread, is another way "to live among us," "to camp with us," "to make his dwelling with us."

This mystery of the faith is a marvel, a miracle of love. It is a free gift, but it is not without its antecedents in the history of salvation. Rather, the eucharistic presence is the culmination of the promise of God whose name is I AM WHO I AM, a God faithful to his covenant, a God always at the side of his people.

In the book of Exodus we read:

> Then the cloud covered the tent of meeting, and the glory of the LORD filled the tabernacle. Moses was not able to enter the tent of meeting because the cloud settled upon it, and the glory of the LORD filled the tabernacle. Whenever the cloud was taken up from the tabernacle, the Israelites would set out on each stage of their journey; but if the cloud was not taken up, then

they did not set out until the day that it was taken up. For the cloud of the LORD was on the tabernacle by day, and fire was in the cloud by night, before the eyes of all the house of Israel at each stage of their journey (Exod 40:34-38).

God was with the people in the desert and the glory of God rested upon God's dwelling place.

Christ in the Blessed Sacrament is with his people and the glory of God is upon us.

The prophet Isaiah saw the Lord seated upon his throne on high. Those beings—angels—around the throne cried out, one after another: "Holy, holy, holy is the LORD of hosts; / the whole earth is full of his glory" (Isa 6:3).

The prophet Isaiah goes on to say: "Woe is me! I am lost, for I am a man of unclean lips, and I live among a people of unclean lips; yet my eyes have seen the King, the LORD of hosts!" (Isa 6:5).

Again here, there is the belief that to look upon the face of God is to die. We mere mortals feel unworthy to be in the presence of God. What is most outstanding is the holiness and the glory of God.

We say the same when we repeat so often in the *Sanctus* of the Mass:

> Holy, holy, holy, Lord God of Hosts!
> Heaven and earth are full of your glory!
> Hosanna in the highest!
> Blessed is he who comes in the name of the Lord.
> Hosanna in the highest!

I make my own the prayer of Isaiah, here before the Blessed Sacrament. Here is the dwelling of God.

Holy, holy, holy!
Hosanna in the highest!

CHAPTER FIFTEEN

The Wedding of Cana

How often have I heard or read about the miracles of Jesus.

The Gospel of Saint John speaks about the "signs" of Christ, "miraculous signs." The miracles of Jesus are not simply tricks in the style of a magician. They were not performed to achieve higher "ratings" or to make impressive images on television. Miracles served as pedagogy in teaching, to make present the saving work of God at a precise moment in the wandering ministry of Jesus. Miracles are revelatory acts of God, are signs of salvation.

The miracle of Jesus at the wedding of Cana is well known. Jesus, reacting to the plea of Mary, his mother, changed water into wine so that the wedding feast could go on.

The Gospel of John says: "Jesus did this, the first of his signs, in Cana of Galilee, and revealed his glory; and his disciples believed in him" (John 2:11).

Every miracle retains an intrinsic relation with faith and conversion. The glory of God, the Father of Jesus, was revealed, and at the miraculous sign of changing water into wine "his disciples believed in him."

All creation is full of the glory of God. It is manifest at the first light of dawn, in the song of birds, in the smile of a child, in the love of grandparents. The glory of God is announced to me in all of creation. I am not a pure spirit, an angel, to whom God communicates directly in a spiritual manner within my soul. God communicates with me through material things. Jesus connected with the people at the wedding feast by changing water into wine. In some physical way the glory of God is made known to all human creatures.

All the sacraments are of material things and of outward actions which are the means by which they make present and active the saving grace of God. The word "sacramentality" has a very profound meaning for Catholics. Sacramentality means that all of creation is in some way a sacrament of God. All of creation is a manifestation of God: the sun, the moon, the countryside, the flowers, the birds—all reveal the glory of God.

Of course, in the Catholic tradition there are those very special material signs: the seven sacraments. But there are also other material things and actions that are called the sacramentals. The most common of the Catholic sacramentals are statues, holy water, blessed metals, rosaries, crosses, scapulars, palms, grottoes, and many more. Sacramentals are material things, once blessed by a minister of the Church, which make present the glory, the holiness, the protection of God.

In the miracle of the wedding of Cana water was changed into wine. No believing Catholic can fail to see in this teaching moment of Jesus an anticipation of the eucharistic miracle where wine is changed into the Blood of Christ.

The Blessed Sacrament is not at all a simple sacramental. Here in the Sacred Host is present Christ himself.

In the Eucharist there is revealed the glory of God. It is a material thing, bread, a sign, but bread transformed into the mystery of faith.

"And his disciples believed in him—Jesus."

I, before the Blessed Sacrament, believe in him.

CHAPTER SIXTEEN

Bread in the Wilderness

Give us this day our daily bread.

An important figure of the Eucharist in the Old Testament is the figure of the miraculous bread in the wilderness: the manna. Many translations speak of the wilderness, but this is not a forest or jungle wilderness. It was a dry, inhospitable desert.

We read in Exodus 16:

> The whole congregation of the Israelites complained against Moses and Aaron in the wilderness. The Israelites said to them, "If only we had died by the hand of the LORD in the land of Egypt, when we sat by the fleshpots and ate our fill of bread; for you have brought us out into this wilderness to kill this whole assembly with hunger."
>
> Then the LORD said to Moses, "I am going to rain bread from heaven for you, and each day the people shall go out and gather enough for that day. In that

way I will test them, whether they will follow my in-
struction or not."

The LORD spoke to Moses and said, "I have heard
the complaining of the Israelites: say to them, 'At twi-
light you shall eat meat, and in the morning you shall
have your fill of bread; then you shall know that I am
the LORD your God.'"

In the evening quails came up and covered the
camp; and in the morning there was a layer of dew
around the camp. When the layer of dew lifted, there
on the surface of the wilderness was a fine flaky sub-
stance, as fine as frost on the ground. When the Israelites saw it, they said to one another, "What is it?"
[manna] For they did not know what it was. Moses
said to them, "It is the bread that the LORD has given
you to eat" (Exod 16:2-4, 11-15).

Give us this day our daily bread.

In the Lord's Prayer, the Our Father, Jesus taught us
that we have the same cry as the people in the wilderness. Give us this day our daily bread.

The miraculous bread in the wilderness was sufficient only for one day.

"This is what the LORD commanded: 'Gather as much
of it as each of you needs, an omer to a person according to the number of persons, all providing for those
in their own tents.'" The Israelites did so, some gather-
ing more, some less. But when they measured it with
an omer, those who gathered much had nothing over,
and those who gathered little had no shortage; they
gathered as much as each of them needed. And Moses
said to them, "Let no one leave any of it over until
morning." But they did not listen to Moses; some left

part of it until morning, and it bred worms and became foul. And Moses was angry with them (Exod 16:16-20).

In his Sermon on the Mount in the Gospel of Saint Matthew, Jesus echoes this lesson of the bread (manna) in the wilderness.

> Therefore I tell you, do not worry about your life, what you will eat or what you will drink, or about your body, what you will wear. . . . Your heavenly Father knows that you need all these things. But strive first for the kingdom of God and his righteousness, and all these things will be given to you as well.
>
> So do not worry about tomorrow, for tomorrow will bring worries of its own. Today's trouble is enough for today (Matt 6:25, 32-34).

Give us this day our daily bread.

Give food for all families, work for the unemployed, medicines for the sick.

I am not to worry myself with anxiety and fear. I am to trust in Divine Providence that feeds the birds of the heavens and clothes the lilies of the fields. Will not the God who so clothes the grass of the field also take care of me and my necessities? Or am I a person of little faith? This is the same God, the Father, I AM WHO I AM, who fed his people in the wilderness with the miraculous bread of manna. Will he perchance forget all about me?

Give us this day our daily bread.

Nevertheless, Jesus also tells us: "One does not live by bread alone, / but by every word that comes from the mouth of God" (Matt 4:4). In the Gospel of Saint John, after the miracle of the multiplication of bread in the countryside, Jesus says: "I am the living bread that came down from heaven." Then Jesus makes direct reference to the bread of the wilderness: "This is the bread that came down from heaven, not like that which your ancestors ate, and they died. But the one who eats this bread will live forever" (John 6:51, 58).

The eucharistic bread giving us the presence of Christ is a profound mystery, a gift beyond all hoping and totally unmerited. Nevertheless, there are various anticipations of the Eucharist in the history of salvation. The manna, the bread in the wilderness, was food directly from heaven. It was food for every day and food sufficient for the day.

Give us this day our daily bread.

Give me the living bread, the Body of Christ every day of my life.

The word "manna" in Hebrew means "What is it?"

It is the living bread, Christ in the sacrament of the altar, here present for me.

This miraculous bread is the love of God made bread in the person of Jesus.

Give us this day our daily bread.

CHAPTER SEVENTEEN

The Ark of the Covenant

God is here.

On Mount Sinai, God appeared in all his glory under the appearance of a dense cloud. The book of Exodus says: "Now the appearance of the glory of the LORD was like a devouring fire on the top of the mountain in the sight of the people off Israel" (Exod 24:17).

This same glory of God and the cloud appeared also in the meeting tent: "When Moses entered the tent, the pillar of cloud would descend and stand at the entrance of the tent, and the LORD would speak with Moses" (Exod 33:9).

Today God is here in the Blessed Sacrament of the altar. Christ as sacrament is present in the eucharistic bread. There are lighted candles, there is the sanctuary lamp, there is the smell of incense. There is something here of the glory of God. And we say: "Holy, holy, holy!"

In the meeting tent there was the ark of the covenant. The ark was made of wood. It was portable. It was something like a carrying platform for statues. The people of Israel carried along with them the ark during the forty years they wandered in the desert wilderness. God accompanied the people, a column of smoke during the day and a column of fire during the night.

When crossing the River Jordan to enter into the Promised Land, the book of Joshua says:

> When the people set out from their tents to cross over the Jordan, the priests bearing the ark of the covenant were in front of the people. . . . The waters flowing from above stood still, rising up in a single heap far off. . . . Then the people crossed over opposite Jericho. While all Israel were crossing over on dry ground, the priests who bore the ark of the covenant of the LORD stood on dry ground in the middle of the Jordan, until the entire nation finished crossing over the Jordan (Josh 3:14, 16-17).

The ark of the covenant was with the people of Israel in all its battles in the conquest of Canaan. For example, in the famous battle of Jericho:

> As Joshua had commanded the people, the seven priests carrying the seven trumpets of rams' horns before the LORD went forward, blowing the trumpets, with the ark of the covenant of the LORD following them. . . . To the people Joshua gave this command: "You shall not shout or let your voice be heard, nor shall you utter a word, until the day I tell you to shout. Then you shall shout." So the ark of the LORD went around the city, circling it. . . . They did this for six days. . . .
>
> On the seventh day they rose early, at dawn, and marched around the city in the same manner seven

times. It was only on that day that they marched around the city seven times. And at the seventh time, when the priests had blown the trumpets, Joshua said to the people, "Shout! For the LORD has given you the city. . . ." So the people shouted, and the trumpets were blown . . . and the wall fell down flat (Josh 6:8, 10-11, 14-16, 20).

The God who appeared to Moses in the burning bush said to him: I AM WHO I AM.

He is a faithful God, a God-with-us, a God always at the side of the people.

After the construction of the Temple by Solomon on Mount Zion in Jerusalem the ark of the covenant was placed in the third part of the Temple, elevated, in the place called the Holy of Holies, behind long, heavy curtains.

In Hebrews 9 we read:

> Now even the first covenant had regulations for worship and an earthly sanctuary. For a tent was constructed, the first one, in which were the lampstand, the table, and the bread of the Presence; this is called the Holy Place. Behind the second curtain was a tent, called the Holy of Holies. In it stood the golden altar of incense, and the ark of the covenant overlaid on all sides with gold, in which there were a golden urn holding the manna, and Aaron's rod that budded, and the tablets of the covenant; above it were the cherubim of glory overshadowing the mercy seat (Heb 9:1-5).

In the ark of the covenant, over and above the rod of Aaron, there was conserved the two tablets of stone of the Ten Commandments and a few pieces of that miraculous bread of the wilderness, manna, which God had given to the people of Israel in the desert.

All of this is a figure, an anticipation of the Liturgy of the Eucharist. There are two parts in the Mass: the Liturgy of the Word—signified by the two stone tablets of the Ten Commandments—and the Liturgy of the Eucharist—signified by the loaves of bread, the manna.

In the wilderness the people of Israel felt the presence of God in the meeting tent; they felt the glory of God in the cloud that was above the ark of the covenant.

In the Temple of Jerusalem for many centuries the Jews felt the presence of God in the Holy of Holies where only the high priest could enter.

I am part of the new people of God. I feel the presence of God in the eucharistic bread, the Body and Blood of Christ, the blood of the new and everlasting covenant.

In faith and adoration I proclaim: God is here!

CHAPTER EIGHTEEN

Christ, the Propitiation for Our Sins

According to the dictionary, to expiate is "to extinguish some incurred guilt through sacred rites or to make amends through the paying of a penalty or the offering of a gift." Usually, a person of faith, feeling the guilt of sin, makes expiation to God.

The biblical concept of expiation is very complex. In the Old Testament the priests were to offer sacrifices of animals to God in order "to expiate" the people's sins and transgressions.

To understand these rites we must return to the construction of the ark of the covenant and how this model was made large in the temple. The tabernacle was a wooden box in which there were preserved the two stone tablets of the Ten Commandments, the miraculous rod of Aaron, and some of the loaves of the miraculous bread of the wilderness, the manna. The lid of the ark was covered with solid gold. On the four corners of the ark there were four golden cherubim. ("Cherubim" is the Hebrew form of the plural of "cherub.") The cherubim were depicted as winged creatures with feet and hands. Over the ark the wings of the four cherubim extended toward the center.

The golden lid of the ark was called the "the propitiatory," or "the place of atonement." Now the translation is "mercy's seat."

Let us repeat the first five verses of Hebrews 9:

> Now even the first covenant had regulations for worship and an earthly sanctuary. For a tent was constructed, the first one, in which were the lampstand, the table, and the bread of the Presence; this is called the Holy Place. Behind the second curtain was a tent [or tabernacle] called the Holy of Holies. In it stood the golden altar of incense and the ark of the covenant overlaid on all sides with gold, in which there were a golden urn holding the manna, and Aaron's rod that budded, and the tablets of the covenant; above it were the cherubim of glory overshadowing the mercy seat [or the place of atonement] (Heb 9:1-5).

Once a year the high priest entered this third part of the Temple, behind the curtains to enter into the Holy of Holies, carrying the blood of the animals that had been sacrificed over the altar in the second part of the Temple. The priest sprinkled the blood upon "the propitiatory," over and above the wings of the cherubim, the mercy seat. Through this rite of expiation God pardoned the sins of the priest and the sins of the people of God. "Indeed, under the law almost everything is purified with blood, and without the shedding of blood there is no forgiveness of sins" (Heb 9:22).

Let me recall again the blood of the first covenant as it is related in the Letter to the Hebrews:

> Hence not even the first covenant was inaugurated without blood. For when every commandment had been told to all the people by Moses in accordance with the law, he took the blood of calves and goats, with water and scarlet wool and hyssop, and sprinkled both the scroll itself and all the people, saying, "This is the blood of the covenant that God has ordained for you." And in the same way he sprinkled with the blood both the tent and the vessels used in worship. Indeed, under the law almost everything is purified with blood, and without the shedding of blood there is no forgiveness of sin (Heb 9:18-22).

But the Letter to the Hebrews also states: "They [the priests of the Old Testament] offer worship in a sanctuary that is a sketch and shadow of the heavenly one" (Heb 8:5).

"Since the law has only a shadow of the good things to come and not the true form of these realities, it can never, by the same sacrifices that are continually offered year after year, make perfect those who approach" (Heb 10:1).

Then the letter gives the reason:

> For this reason he [Christ] is the mediator of a new covenant, so that those who are called may receive the promised eternal inheritance, because a death has occurred that redeems them from the transgressions under the first covenant (Heb 9:15).

>The high priest enters the Holy Place year after year
>with blood that is not his own (Heb 9:25).

>But when Christ came as a high priest of the good
>things that have come . . . he entered once and for all
>into the Holy Place, not with the blood of goats and
>calves, but with his own blood, thus obtaining eternal
>redemption. For if the blood of goats and bulls, with
>the sprinkling of the ashes of a heifer, sanctifies those
>who have been defiled so that their flesh is purified,
>how much more will the blood of Christ, who through
>the eternal Spirit offered himself without blemish to
>God, purify our conscience from dead works to wor-
>ship the saving God! (Heb 9:11-14).

How much more the blood of Christ! All the rites,
the sacrifices, and the traditions of the Old Testament
are now obsolete. Now in Christ there is a new cult, a
new covenant, a new sense of authentic worship.

"And every priest stands day after day at his service,
offering again and again the same sacrifices that can
never take away sins. But when Christ had offered for
all time a single sacrifice for sins . . ." (Heb 10:11-12).

With this one and only sacrifice (that is to say, the
offering of himself, the offering of his will and of his
own blood), "by a single offering he [Christ] has per-
fected for all time those who are sanctified. . . . Where
there is forgiveness of these, there is no longer any offering for sin" (Heb 10:14, 18).

Christ is the expiation for my sins. I am pardoned by
the blood of Christ poured out on the cross in a way similar to how the blood of animals had been sprinkled over
the "mercy seat" in the Holy of Holies in the Temple.

In the Eucharist, Christ is present permanently in the one and only act of sacrifice to God the Father. Christ sanctifies me through baptism and then through my faith perfects me because the blood of Christ is "propitiation," is "atonement" before God.

And my sins are forgiven.

CHAPTER NINETEEN

Christ, the One and Only Sacrifice

In the wilderness God made his dwelling in the meeting tent outside the camp of the people of Israel. It was there that one felt the presence of God. Especially was God felt to be present when Moses entered the tent to speak intimately with God.

"Then the cloud covered the tent of meeting, and the glory of the LORD filled the tabernacle. Moses was not able to enter the tent of meeting because the cloud settled upon it, and the glory of the LORD filled the tabernacle" (Exod 40:34-35).

We have seen how in the prologue of the Gospel of John what is traditionally expressed as "He dwelt among us" or "He lived among us" should be translated as "He camped with us," "He put up his tent in our camp." The following words are found in the same verse of Saint John: "And we have seen his glory, the glory as of a father's only son, full of grace and truth"

(John 1:14). Now, in this Holy Hour, Christ has his dwelling here. He is present in the eucharistic bread.

I feel the glory of God. The scent and the smoke of incense in the church help me to imagine the dark cloud that covers the face of God. In faith I see "the glory as of a father's only son, full of grace and truth."

It is difficult to reconstruct the sanctuary in the desert wilderness, because the descriptions we read in the book of Exodus are, for the most part, descriptions of the Temple of Jerusalem. It would seem that the tent of meeting was a small scale temple, divided into two parts, the holy place and the "most holy" place—the Holy of Holies. We have seen that there are many names for this place. It would seem that the best name is "the tent of presence," because God was present in this place.

From the moment of the incarnation of God in Christ, the moment when "the Word became flesh," God is present with the human family in the humanity of Christ. The Letter to the Hebrews says: "Consequently, when Christ came into the world, he said [and with references to Psalm 40], 'Sacrifices and offerings you have not desired; / but a body you have prepared for me'" (Heb 10:5).

This is not simply an organic body; this is the incarnation of God in Jesus. In the same passage the Letter to the Hebrews repeats the words of Psalm 40. "Then I said, 'See, God, I have come to do your will, O God'" (Heb 10:7). And it continues: "And it is by God's will that we have been sanctified through the offering of the body of Jesus Christ once for all" (Heb 10:10).

Here is the key to our salvation. Christ one time and for all offered to God in sacrifice his body and blood for the forgiveness of our sins. As the high priest had to pass through the curtains of the Temple with the blood of animals, by his humanity the body of Christ is like a veil or curtain and "we have confidence to enter the sanctuary by the blood of Jesus" (Heb 10:19).

> But when Christ came as a high priest of the good things that have come, then through the greater and perfect tent (not made with hands, that is not of this creation) he entered once for all into the Holy Place, not with the blood of goats and calves, but with his own blood, thus obtaining eternal redemption (Heb 9:11-12).

The Eucharist is the "tent" of the presence of God for the new people of Israel.

The Eucharist is the permanent presence of the one sacrifice of Christ, offered once and for all.

The Eucharist is the presence of the same liberating God who had always stayed present with the first people of Israel.

But most of all, the Eucharist is the permanent presence of the one sacrifice of Christ, the High Priest by excellence, who offered his own blood to God the Father.

"And it is by God's will that we have been sanctified through the offering of the body of Jesus Christ once for all" (Heb 10:10).

CHAPTER TWENTY

Advent

Advent means "coming." Now he is coming. It is definite and certain that he is near.

All of Advent is like a Holy Hour. It is a vigil, a watching, a moment of hope, to prepare myself, to open my heart to the action of the Holy Spirit, the way Mary did at the annunciation of the archangel Gabriel.

In the Gospels Jesus tells his disciples: "Keep awake therefore, for you do not know on what day your Lord is coming. . . . Therefore you also must be ready, for the Son of Man is coming at an unexpected hour" (Matt 24:42, 44). "Beware, keep alert; for you do not know when the time will come" (Mark 13:33).

In a certain sense this is the attitude of contemplation. "Keep awake!" "Keep alert!" God is here. The reign of God has come. Therefore, attention! No one knows when the owner of the house will return!

The mystery of the sacrament of the Eucharist is at this very point. Yes, Jesus, my Savior, has come some two thousand years ago. He is my life and my salvation. I adore Jesus present in the Sacred Host. Come, Lord Jesus! Christ is present in the profound mystery of the sacrament.

By faith, I believe in the presence of Christ in the Blessed Sacrament. It is through faith and only faith. I do not actually see what I profess in faith. The mystery is what is beyond and below of that which I touch, that which I taste in the bread. Christ is present in the profound mystery of the sacrament.

I am making a vigil. I am awake, alert, watching like the prudent virgins, with my lamp burning to receive Christ the bridegroom when he comes.

Christ will come one day in the fullness of his power and glory. My faith gives me this hope.

Even though Christ is now present, yet he delays in his second coming. "Come, Lord Jesus!"

The reign of God is within me and I pray: "Thy kingdom come."

Another reason why I feel this ambiguity of the faith is the fact that I am a sinner. Some lines of Psalm 79:

> How long, O LORD? Will you be angry forever?
>   Will your jealous wrath burn like fire?
> Do not remember against us the iniquities of our
>   ancestors;
>   let your compassion come speedily to meet us,
>   for we are brought very low.
> Help us, O God of our salvation,
>   for the glory of your name;

> deliver us, and forgive our sins,
>> for your name's sake (Ps 79:5, 8-9).

Therefore, Advent is a time of conversion. Convert! The reign of God is near.

Advent is the time of salvation.

He is coming! Who is coming? The Messiah, the Anointed One, the Savior!

"The angel said to her, 'Do not be afraid, Mary, for you have found favor with God. And now, you will conceive in your womb and bear a son, and you will name him Jesus'" (Luke 1:30-31).

The name Jesus means "Savior," he who saves me from my sins.

Now he is certainly coming. This is Advent. Do not be afraid.

This is the attitude of contemplation.

CHAPTER TWENTY-ONE

The Beginning and the End

(Advent/Christmas)

In the book of Revelation Jesus says, "I am the Alpha and the Omega, the first and the last, the beginning and the end" (Rev 22:13). The last words of the last book of the Bible are: "'Surely I am coming soon.' Amen. Come, Lord Jesus! The grace of the Lord Jesus be with all the saints. Amen" (Rev 22:20-21).

In the Church of San Francisco de Borja in Lima, Peru, there is on the high wall of the sanctuary behind the altar a huge mosaic of the New Jerusalem. Above are written the Greek letters Alpha, Omega. These are the first and the last letters of the Greek alphabet. To the right, above the tabernacle of the Blessed Sacrament, there is a wood carving of the Christ of the Apocalypse, holding in his hands the book of life which reads: "Surely, I am coming soon."

The words "beginning" and "end" are ambiguous. We are not to understand that the Word of God has had a beginning and will have an end. This is not its meaning. We should understand the phrase to say that I am without beginning and I will have no end. As we say in the prayer of the "Glory be to the Father" and in many other prayers: "As it was in the beginning, is now, and will be forever, world without end." "World without end" means forever, everlasting, without limit, for all eternity. This is why we say: "Eternal Father": God without beginning and without end.

In the Prologue of the Gospel of Saint John we have seen: "In the beginning was the Word, and the Word was with God, and the Word was God" (John 1:1).

"In the beginning . . . ." Now, this does not mean that there was a beginning. Rather, here "beginning" means "forever," "from all eternity," "in the beyond where there is no beginning." From eternity and on to all of eternity has the Word existed because the Word was God.

In verse 14 of the Prologue Saint John says, "And the Word became flesh and lived among us." We have seen that his "dwelling among us" has reference to the meeting tent, the tabernacle of the Old Testament: the tent outside of the camp of the people of God in the wilderness where God stayed with the people as a pillar of smoke by day and a pillar of fire by night.

In the Incarnation of the Word of God, this same Word took on our human nature, became flesh, bone, and blood. He "put up his tent" in our own camp. He dwelt among us.

The eternal Word took on the condition of a mortal, decided to be equal to me, took on the whole of the human condition. He was born of Mary, a young maiden recently married to Joseph.

Jesus of Nazareth, YES, does have a beginning and an end. The Virgin conceived her child the moment she answered the archangel Gabriel "Here am I, the servant of the Lord; let it be with me according to your word" (Luke 1:38).

> We believe in Jesus Christ,
> his only Son, Our Lord.
> He was conceived by the power of the Holy Spirit
> and born of the Virgin Mary.

Christmas is the birthday of Jesus, the anniversary of his birth in the flesh. This is the point of the mystery. The eternal Word without beginning enters into our historical time, into our human time.

The Eucharist touches profoundly this mystery of the Incarnation. "The Word is made flesh." Christ is made bread.

Since the birth of the Child Jesus we mark the passing of time—the days, the weeks, the years, the centuries, the millenniums from the moment of his birth. Now it has been more than two thousand years since he was born of the flesh. He who is the eternal Word, who is and has been and will be "worlds without end." He, the son of Mary.

The Word entered into our time. Two thousand years have passed. He who is without beginning and without end dwells with us.

Today, here, I am in the presence of this mystery, before the Word of God made flesh, made bread for us. I have no words. I remain in silence, overcome, overwhelmed, grateful.

I hear him who says:

"I am the Alpha and the Omega, the first and the last, the beginning and the end."

"I am about to come."

"Amen." "Lord Jesus, come."

"Come, Lord Jesus."

CHAPTER TWENTY-TWO

"Let us go up to the house of the Lord"

(Liturgical Psalms 14; 15; 91; 122; 134, among others)

The psalms are poems, prayers inspired by the Holy Spirit. The Church has always regarded the psalms as the best expressions of how to pray to God. The psalms can be read and prayed at various levels: as poetry, as history, as expressions of a culture. Some psalms are hymns to God, the Creator and Lord. Others are hymns to the Lord as King and Warrior. Some psalms are hymns to Zion/Jerusalem and to the Temple. There are pilgrim psalms, psalms of petitions, of thanksgiving. There are historical psalms, prophetic psalms, wisdom psalms.

I can select whatever psalm that corresponds to my feelings of the day: thanksgiving and joy, anxiety and fear, remorse and repentance. I can pray many of the psalms united intimately with Christ, who, of course, prayed the psalms as his daily bread. For example, Psalm 22: "My God, my God, why have you forsaken me!" More correctly, through the fullness of the revelation of God that we have in Christ one can pray all the psalms, one by one, united intimately with Christ.

Here, before the Blessed Sacrament, one can select those psalms that are called pilgrim psalms or liturgical psalms. For example, Psalm 122: "I was glad when they said to me, / 'Let us go to the house of the LORD!'" (Ps 122:1).

There are some fifteen psalms classified as "Pilgrim Psalms." In the Gospel of Saint Luke, in the story of the parents of Jesus, one reads: "Now every year his parents went to Jerusalem for the festival of the Passover. And when he was twelve years old, they went up as usual for the festival" (Luke 2:41-42). The line says "they went up." For its geographical location, Jerusalem as a city is much higher than Galilee and Nazareth. Further, the temple was built upon the high rock overlooking the city, the rock of Zion. That is why the Pilgrim Psalms are called "Ascending Psalms." To get to the temple above the city of Jerusalem one must ascend a number of stairs. The pilgrim ascended slowly, in stages, singing and praising God.

> I was glad when they said to me,
> "Let us go up to the house of the LORD!"
> Our feet are standing
> within your gates, O Jerusalem (Ps 122:1-2).

For the Jewish people—and for us—a pilgrimage calls to mind the flight from Egypt in the days of the

Exodus. A pilgrimage brings to mind of the people of Israel the exile to Babylon. A pilgrimage is a pre-figuring of the future messianic time when all the nations of the world will go up to Jerusalem.

> Jerusalem—built as a city
>   that is bound firmly together.
> To it the tribes go up,
>   the tribes of the LORD,
> as was decreed for Israel,
>   to give thanks to the name of the LORD (Ps 122:3-4).

The mystery of salvation is always in this historical context. Always our present faith and joy has reference to the past and to the future. "For there the thrones for judgment were set up, / the thrones of the house of David" (Ps 122:5).

There is a looking back to the great King David, while the people seek justice in the tribunals of their own day.

> Pray for the peace of Jerusalem:
>   "May they prosper who love you.
> Peace be within your walls,
>   and security within your towers."
> For the sake of my relatives and friends
>   I will say, "Peace be within you."
> For the sake of the house of the LORD our God,
>   I will seek your good (Ps 122:6-9).

The word for "peace" in Hebrew is *"shalom."* The name of the capital city of the Jewish people is Jerusalem. *"Salem"* is derived from *"shalom."* Jerusalem is the place of peace.

It is a public demonstration of joy to make a pilgrimage to Jerusalem to express deep emotions walking through the streets of the Holy City. The pilgrim, joyful and thankful, calls down a benediction and prays for peace upon the city.

During the Holy Year 2000 there were many pilgrimages to Rome from all parts of the world, as well as to the Holy Land. It is the joy of the pilgrim that Psalm 122 sings: "I was glad when they said to me, / 'Let us go up to the house of the LORD!'"

In every Catholic church the Blessed Sacrament is reserved in the tabernacle. The Temple of Jerusalem had its "Holy of Holies," the ark of the covenant with the two stone tablets of the Ten Commandments and loaves of bread from the wilderness. That Temple was holy through the presence of God.

This church where I am today is more holy for the presence of Christ in the Eucharist. Here before the Blessed Sacrament exposed I am before the mystery of Christ, before the reality of my liberation by Christ.

"Peace be within these walls."

May we all live in peace! Peace! Here in the house of the Lord.

Peace in all parts of the world.

CHAPTER TWENTY-THREE

Zen Meditation and the Eucharist

In 1971, Father Ernest Ranly made a journey to the East. He shares with us his story:

> I spent only three months in India, yet the Eastern religions, Hinduism, Buddhism, and Zen, have affected me deeply and permanently in the way I pray, in my method of meditation, and even in some expressions of my faith.
>
> Later I participated in a weekend Zen Buddhist retreat in the United States. The director of the retreat was a Zen Master, whose title is "roshi." (In Hindu the master is called "guru.") Our roshi was a huge Japanese man who spoke only Japanese. The translator was a young, North American Jesuit priest.
>
> The technique of Zen meditation comes from a tradition of some three thousand years. The purpose of the meditation—it would be better to call it contemplation—is to have the practitioner arrive at a sense of complete interior peace, a sense of complete integration of the person's being with all of nature at the

*precise time of meditation. This requires great inter-
nal discipline.*

*In the philosophy of Zen neither the past nor the
future exist. There is only the present, this very moment. The purpose for the control of all emotions and
feelings is to become totally aware of yourself, at this
moment, in this setting, here, now. You must control
your breathing, have discipline over the eyes and over
your thoughts. You think of nothing. You do not speak
a word. You should enter into your own interior, at
this precise moment, with the light that is here, the
sounds. Perhaps you come to feel identified with a
flower, a fallen leaf, a bee passing from flower to
flower. Thus you are in communion with all that is,
that which is called Tao. You begin to lose your own
identity as you feel integrated into the fullness of that
which is the reality of this moment. Only the present,
this moment is that which is. This is the now.*

There are some very interesting, very positive
points in the Zen method of meditation. There are
various aspects that correspond to our eucharistic contemplation.

God is here.

I am before the Blessed Sacrament.

This is a holy place. "Remove your sandals!"

Here and now I feel the glory of God.

It is a moment of silence. Let there be no words.
These are moments of meditation, which we call contemplation, eucharistic contemplation.

But there are great differences between the philosophy and practice of Zen Buddhism and the Catholic
faith and practice. For Zen only the present exists. The

past no longer exists, because it has passed. We should not worry about the past. It is no more.

For Zen the future does not exist. Simply, the future has not happened; it is not in any way here. I cannot know anything about that which does not exist. We ought not to worry about the future, because the future does not exist. We can never know anything about the future.

But what do I have in the Eucharist?

In the Mass, after the consecration, the celebrant says: "Let us proclaim the mystery of faith!" And the people respond: "Christ has died. Christ is risen. Christ will come again."

The mystery of Christ is the fullness of salvation. In this mystery, Christ died for me—the past. He lives now for me—Christ is risen. He will come in glory at the end of the times—Christ will come again.

The discipline of Zen can help us in our eucharistic contemplation. We need internal discipline to control our thoughts, to not fall into distractions or think about financial problems, family problems.

It is also very valuable to have a discipline of breathing, to have a good posture, to help us to be attentive to the mystery of Christ.

This is a Holy Hour.

This is a moment of the Holy Spirit.

This is the moment in which the love of God is present in the Blessed Sacrament.

I must allow the love of God to penetrate into my heart.

Let me live intensely this present moment, because without a present awareness, the past and the future have no meaning for me.

At this moment Christ is present in the eucharistic bread in all his mystery, past, present, and future. In this way the transcendental meditation of Zen Buddhism can be transformed into eucharistic contemplation.

"This is the Sacrament of our faith."

"This is the mystery of faith."

CHAPTER TWENTY-FOUR

Pope John Paul II
in the Cenacle of Jerusalem

(Holy Thursday—Jubilee Year, 2000)

A moment of great significance in the life of Pope John Paul II was his visit to the Cenacle on Holy Thursday during the Jubilee Year 2000. From that upper room the Holy Father wrote his traditional letter to all the priests of the world with the motive to commemorate the anniversary of the institution of the priesthood during the Last Supper, which, according to tradition, took place in that very place, in the Cenacle of Jerusalem.

The Pope wrote:

> I am re-reading with great emotion, here in Jerusalem, in this place, in which, according to tradition, there were present Jesus and the Twelve for the pur-

pose to celebrate the Pascal Supper and the Institution of the Eucharist.

"Jesus having loved his own loved them to the end" (John 13:1). With these words the evangelist John begins the narration of the Last Supper.

And the Holy Father continues: "Today, this visit to the Cenacle gives me the opportunity to contemplate the mystery of redemption in all its dimensions. It was here that Christ gave us the immeasurable gift of the Eucharist. Here there was born our priesthood."

In my Holy Hour, my Cenacle is the Blessed Sacrament here exposed. The Pope exhorts all the priests of the world: We should prostrate ourselves frequently and for a long time in adoration before Christ in the Eucharist. We should enter, in some way, into "the school of the Eucharist."

"In the school of the Eucharist" John Paul II, teacher within the magisterium of the Church, teaches me a number of lessons. He writes: "Here in the Cenacle there began for the world a new presence of Christ. . . . This Eucharistic presence has been passed down in the Church for two millenniums and will be with the Church until the end of History."

He says in another place:

> The Eucharistic action . . . will be made present in every Christian generation, in every corner of the earth, the work realized by Christ. In every place in which there is celebrated the Eucharist, there, as a type of encounter, there will be present the bloody sacrifice of Calvary, there will be present the same Christ, Redeemer of the world.

And so, I repeat, my Cenacle is right here, at this moment. Christ himself, redeemer of the world, is present here.

Another lesson which the Holy Father teaches is that the Eucharist is not simply a reminder, but a memorial that is brought about; the Eucharist is not simply a symbolic return to the past, but it is a living presence of the Savior in our midst. For this there is always the guarantee of the Holy Spirit whose coming in the eucharistic celebration changes the bread and wine into the Body and Blood of Christ. It is the same Spirit which, on the night of Easter Sunday, in this Cenacle, was "breathed upon the apostles." And it was here again he met them united with Mary on the day of Pentecost.

That is to say, the first day of the week, the day of the Resurrection, when it was evening the disciples had met—and by tradition it was this same Cenacle—and the doors of the house were locked for fear of the Jews. Jesus came and stood among them and said, "Peace be with you." When he said this he breathed on them and said to them, "Receive the Holy Spirit" (John 20:19, 20). Saint Luke writes in the Acts of the Apostles: "When the day of Pentecost had come, they were all together in one place" (Acts 2:1)—that it is to say, writes John Paul II, in the same Cenacle.

The Holy Father has good reasons for being so emotionally moved by being in such a holy place.

A third lesson of the Pope is the intimate relation between the mystery of the incarnation of the Word and of the sacrament of the Eucharist, the sacrament of the real presence of Christ. That is to say: The Word of God who became flesh and lived among us is the same Christ of the Sacrament. The fullness of the mystery of Christ is present in the Eucharist.

I have here my own Cenacle.

Where the Blessed Sacrament is exposed and the faithful are in adoration there is present Christ in the Cenacle with his disciples.

CHAPTER TWENTY-FIVE

Grace, the Fullness of the Christian Life

How rare—and how wonderful—that Christ is present here in the Sacred Host!

It is only with faith that I can approach the mystery of Christ with the certainty that he is here: Christ now, yesterday, and forever. This very faith is a free gift of God.

My first prayer is one of thanksgiving for the gift of faith that I have so that I can adore Christ in the sacrament of the Eucharist.

God created the world freely and out of love. I am a creature of God, made according to his image and likeness. I am a very special creation of God. The book of Genesis speaks of the seven days of creation. In the first five days God says: The first day: "Let there be light." The second day: "Let there be a dome—the sky." The third day: "Let there be earth and water and vegetation." The fourth day: "Let the sun rule over the day and the moon to rule over the night." The fifth day: "Fill the waters in the sea with living creatures and let the birds fill the air and let the earth bring forth living creatures of all kind" (see Gen 1:4-24). "God saw everything that he had made, and indeed, it was very good" (Gen 1:31).

The sixth day was very special. It was as if God thought for a while and then decided for a special creation on top of everything he had made.

> Then God said, "Let us make humankind in our image, according to our likeness. . . ."
>> So God created humankind in his image,
>> in the image of God he created them;
>> male and female he created them (Gen 1:26, 27).

The second chapter of the book of Genesis has another account of God's creation. "Then the LORD God formed man from the dust of the ground, and breathed into his nostrils the breath of life; and the man became a living being" (Gen 2:7). Later, God called this man Adam and his helper Eve.

This means that I am a very special creature of God. I am a person. Not only am I created, I am called by God with a name. In me God breathed a soul, "the breath of life," something proper only to Spirit.

I accept this account from the book of Genesis in faith. This is not an explanation from the natural sciences, such as biology or geology; nor is it philosophy, as such. Yet from this time forward the human family has a very special relation with God. The first article of the Apostles' Creed is a statement of faith and not a truth of science: "We believe in one God, Father Almighty, Creator of Heaven and Earth."

What is more, I, a sinner, child of Adam and Eve, have been redeemed by the precious blood of Christ. Through my baptism I was reborn a child of God. From that moment I have a new dignity, a new reality. In the rite of baptism the minister places a white cloth over the baptized and says: "This white vestment is a sign of the dignity of a Christian."

Baptism and faith are only a beginning, an entrance, into a new, sacred existence. This is called the grace of God, the life of the Holy Trinity within my own being.

To the extent that I am a believing Christian, I am somehow touched by the mystery of the grace of God in my soul. The grace of God is a free gift. It can never be merited, never be deserved. God is God and only God can give himself in love to me.

When I, with faith, with love, with hope, enter into this relation with God there is realized something in me which does not come from me. It comes only from God.

Faith, hope, charity are the theological virtues. It would be better to say that they are "divine" and "infused" virtues, because through them the life of God is realized in me.

For me to approach the Blessed Sacrament I must leave behind my senses, my human way of knowing. I approach the Sacred Host only with faith.

For this reason, before the Blessed Sacrament it is easier for me to enter profoundly into my own inner being where I encounter the life of God within me.

Eucharistic contemplation is a profoundly human activity, but it is also beyond what is merely human. Only the believer, from the mystery of faith, can encounter Christ in the Eucharist.

The Christian life is something beyond a life enclosed only within the senses.

Eucharistic adoration is only possible with a Christian who is in contact with the most profound depths of the soul.

Eucharistic faith is something beyond the daily life of simply being a Christian.

CHAPTER TWENTY-SIX

The Eucharist
Where There Is No Eucharist

Again the Blessed Sacrament is exposed. God is here in the figure of the sacred bread of the host. The love of God is present in the person of his only Son who died and rose from the dead for me. The Christian community makes memorial of all this every day until Christ comes again.

I count my blessings and I give thanks to God for all he gives me. There are relatively few people in the world who have the good fortune to participate in daily Mass and a weekly Holy Hour. God is good!

Father Ernest Ranly wants to share some notes he wrote while taking part in a series of missions in the deep jungles of Peru:

> *I write these lines in the Peruvian jungle on a small launch on the Ucayali River. We are almost at the halfway mark between Iquitos and Pucallpa, travel-*

ing on the launch *La Granada*, which is the property
of the apostolic vicariate of Requena. We are part of a
Mission Team to accompany Monsignor Victor de la
Peña, a Franciscan priest, bishop-missionary of this
large area for the last thirty years.

It is Sunday afternoon. This morning we concluded
our missionary visits at two settlements. At one place
we baptized twelve people during Mass. At the other
settlement there were more baptisms and a wedding.
Tomorrow, Monday, we are to go to another settlement on the other side of the Ucayali River.

I am thinking of our eucharistic Holy Hours, thinking
about the Eucharist where there is no Eucharist.

We of this missionary team celebrate Mass daily,
at 7:00 in the evening, in the dining room of *La
Granada*. These are very special moments. Monsignor
Victor makes references to our pastoral work with the
people of these settlements, their poverty, their humil-
ity, and their good will. Every day we have for ourselves the Supper that Jesus had with his disciples. It is
dark outside the boat. There is the noise of thousands
of frogs, birds, insects. It is very hot inside the dining
room. The Mass is shared with mosquitoes and gnats
that bother us and we slap at them and kill them. The
moving current of the river rocks the boat like a
baby's cradle.

And Christ is with us. He who went through all
parts of the countryside doing good; Christ who so
often ate with friends and with sinners. He shares his
Body and Blood with us.

We have the Eucharist every day. And our people?
In these parts, missionaries visit the settlements every
two or three years. Faith in the Eucharist, one can
imagine, is very weak. With great enthusiasm the

people sing hymns and other songs. They listen with attention to the Word of God. They beg for baptism. Some youth ask for the sacrament of confirmation. Some receive the sacrament of matrimony. Members of the mission team visit families, offering the sacrament of the sick for the elderly and for the sick.

And the Eucharist? A few children have been prepared for First Communion. But why offer them First Communion if there will be no Mass in their settlement for the next two or three years?

What are we to think about the Eucharist where there is no Eucharist?

In the first place, the mystery of the love of God is the same. "For God so loved the world that he gave his only Son, so that everyone who believes in him may not perish but may have eternal life" (John 3:16). This is a fact equally as true here in the jungle as in any other part of the world. The only Son of God has come in flesh, bone, and blood. Jesus is a near brother to all our brothers and sisters here along these river banks.

In the Eucharist, elements of the earth, the flour of wheat and the juice of grapes, are transformed into the Body and Blood of Christ. We receive bread and wine through God's generosity and the labor of men and women. Here in the jungle we eat yucca—the root of a tree—the juice of coconuts and sugar cane. But the mystery is the same. The incarnation is a reality in all its fullness, in all parts, for all time. Christ is the only Savior, today, yesterday, and forever.

The mission of the Church is not finished with only hymns and the Word of God. The mission of the Catholic Church is to announce the Kingdom of God to all creation and to bring Christ to all parts. Also, to

*bring Christ in the sacrament of the Eucharist, the
very Sacrifice of the Mass, to all parts of the world.*

Now here am I, in this church, with Christ present
in the sacrament of the altar. This is not simply a privi-
lege. I should unite myself with so many people of the
world where there is no Eucharist. Saint Thérèse of
Lisieux is the patron of missions: she, who never left
her cloistered convent. My eucharistic contemplation
can also be a missionary contemplation.

Through my faith here and through the mystery of
Divine Providence, may there be an extension of the
Eucharist in all those parts where there is no Eucharist.

CHAPTER TWENTY-SEVEN

Bread for the Journey

With the people in the high mountains of Peru, when someone is about to make a journey the family prepares a packet of roasted corn and dry cheese so that the traveler will have something to eat on the way.

Here is a passage from 1 Kings 19:3-8:

> Then he [the prophet Elijah] was afraid; he got up and fled for his life, and came to Beersheba, which belongs to Judah; he left his servant there.
>
> But he himself went a day's journey into the wilderness, and came and sat down under a solitary broom tree. He asked that he might die: "It is enough; now, O LORD, take away my life, for I am no better than my ancestors." Then he lay down under the broom tree and fell asleep. Suddenly an angel touched him and said to him, "Get up and eat." He looked, and there at his head was a cake baked on hot stones, and a jar of water. He ate and drank, and lay down again. The angel of the LORD came a second time, touched

him, and said, "Get up and eat, otherwise the journey
will be too much for you." He got up, and ate and
drank; then he went in the strength of that food forty
days and forty nights to Horeb the mount of God.

Now I want to reflect in silence over this wonderful
passage from the Old Testament.

"Horeb the mount of God" is the place where the
Lord God appeared to Moses in the burning bush and
revealed to him his name YHWH, I AM WHO I AM. It is
the Holy Place where God said to Moses, "Come no
closer! Remove the sandals from your feet, for the
place on which you stand is holy ground."

I am in my Holy Hour before the Blessed Sacrament. This church is holy ground. In my culture I do
not remove my shoes, but, yes, I approach the sacrament with respect and reverence. I am on holy ground.

Elijah went on through the desert wilderness for
forty days and forty nights. This is the same desert
wilderness where Moses and the people of Israel wandered for forty years. At that time God fed the people
with the miraculous bread of the manna. Here an
angel offered Elijah two times a portion of hot baked
bread. With the strength of that food he walked forty
days and forty nights. God looks out after the people
with bread and with strength. Christ looks out after
me with the strength of the eucharistic bread.

Saint Matthew says, "Then Jesus was led up by the
Spirit into the wilderness . . . . He fasted forty days
and forty nights, and afterwards he was famished"
(Matt 4:1-2). As a temptation, the devil asked Jesus to
change stones into bread. Jesus answered: "One does

not live by bread alone, / but by every word that comes from the mouth of God" (Matt 4:4).

Reflecting upon these passages I come to realize that I, too, am a traveler here on earth. I need my bread every day, be it the food of toasted corn and dry cheese or hot baked bread. But much more, I need that spiritual bread which comes from the mouth of God. In Saint John Jesus says: "I am the living bread that came down from heaven. Whoever eats of this bread will live forever" (John 6:51).

The experience of Elijah is my life all over again—and, in some manner, the life of everyone. I go through life with fear, with apprehensions, and I run from one crisis to another. With Elijah I cry out: "Lord! It is enough! Take away my life!"

But in Christ, God does not abandon me. I have here the Blessed Sacrament exposed: "Bread baked and still hot."

Of course, I have so much to do, my work, so many responsibilities. "Get up and eat!"

Christ in the Eucharist gives me the strength to walk "forty days and forty nights," that is, a very long time, an indefinite time, the time that God gives me. "He who eats this bread will live forever."

The Eucharist is bread for the journey.

Representatives of business companies get traveling expenses when making official trips. In Peru they call this special traveling/eating allotment a viaticum. Of course, for Catholics, viaticum is that very special Communion for the dying. The sacrament viaticum is bread for the journey from this mortal life to life everlasting.

In the rites for giving the Eucharist to a dying person the minister says:

> My brothers and sisters:
> Before our Lord Jesus Christ passed from this world to return to his Father, he gave us the sacrament of his body and blood. This is the promise of our resurrection, the food and drink for our journey as we pass from this life to join him. United in the love of Christ, let us ask God to give strength to our sister (brother).

The eucharistic bread is Jesus, the living bread come down from heaven. This is my bread for the journey, for my daily runnings around. With the strength of this spiritual food I can walk, along with Elijah, all the days of my life until I come upon the mountain of God, until I make that final journey to heaven. Amen.

CHAPTER TWENTY-EIGHT

The Eucharist and the Servant of the Lord

(Lent and the Paschal Season)

> Lord, by your cross and resurrection
>   You have set us free.
>   You are the Savior of the World.

This is one of the acclamations made by the people after the consecration of the Mass. But also for me, now, before the exposition of the Blessed Sacrament this is a very effective prayer to repeat slowly and meaningfully. And for all the days of Lent and for the paschal season we can repeat:

> Lord, by your cross and resurrection
>   You have set us free.
>   You are the Savior of the world.

In the Nicene Creed which we pray at Mass we say: "We believe in one Lord, Jesus Christ. . . . For us and for our salvation he became human. . . . For our sake he was crucified under Pontius Pilate, suffered, died and was buried. On the third day he rose again. . . . He ascended into heaven."

This is our faith.

Jesus fulfilled to the very letter the mysterious prophecy in the book of Isaiah that speaks about the servant of YHWH. In the fourth poem or canticle we read:

> Surely he has borne our infirmities
>   and carried our diseases;
> yet we accounted him stricken,
>   struck down by God, and afflicted.
> But he was wounded for our transgressions,
>   crushed for our iniquities;
> upon him was the punishment that made us whole,
>   and by his bruises we are healed.
> All we like sheep have gone astray;
>   we have all turned to our own way,
> and the LORD has laid on him
>   the iniquity of us all (Isa 53:4-6).

The canticle ends with supposedly the words of God:

> The righteous one, my servant,
>   shall make many righteous,
> and he shall bear their iniquities. . . .
> He bore the sin of many,
>   and made intercession for the transgressors
>   (Isa 53:11-12).

The disciples of Jesus understood the passion, death, and resurrection of Jesus as the fulfillment of this prophecy in Isaiah about the person the servant of YHWH. The accounts of the passion and death of Jesus in the four Gospels are a reflection of the four poems/canticles of the servant of YHWH in the book of Isaiah.

Jesus, walking with the two disciples to Emmaus on the very day of his resurrection, the first day of the week, explains to them: "Oh, how foolish you are and how slow of heart to believe all that the prophets have declared! Was it not necessary that the Messiah should suffer these things and then enter into his glory?" (Luke 24:25).

The mystery of our redemption is so profound and complex that it is impossible to keep the whole mystery into only one focus. Therefore, there is no limit to our eucharistic contemplation. Oh, Christ, you gave yourself up for us!

From these prophecies of Isaiah "we/us" is that group of people who deserve suffering and punishments. "All we like sheep have gone astray; / we have all turned to our own way" (Isa 53:6).

I am overwhelmed by the mystery of the love of God for me. I am that sheep gone astray, a sinner, guilty. But the servant of the Lord, my Lord Jesus, suffers for me. "He was wounded for our transgressions, crushed for our iniquities; upon him was the punishment that made us whole, and by his bruises we are healed."

These words are not simply written in some obscure book of the Old Testament. Here before the Blessed Sacrament I have these same sentiments. That which was foretold in Isaiah was fulfilled by Jesus—in the past—and is present now in the eucharistic presence. I look at Christ in the eucharistic bread, at the one "who by his bruises we are healed."

In another verse we read:

> Yet it was the will of the LORD to crush him with pain.
> When you make his life an offering for sin,
>   he shall see his offspring and shall prolong his days;
> through him the will of the LORD shall prosper (Isa
>   53:10).

We have noted earlier that "an offering for sin" is an expiation, to expiate for our sins. But also, here we have references not only to the suffering and death of Jesus but also to his resurrection and to the salvation of all the peoples of the world for all times. All this "was the will of the Lord." "Was it not necessary that the Messiah should suffer these things and then enter into his glory?"

> Lord, by your cross and resurrection
> you have set us free.
> You are the savior of the world.

CHAPTER TWENTY-NINE

The Eucharist
and Our Lord of Miracles

In the city of Lima, all along the coast, and practically in all of Peru there is deep faith and profound devotion in honor of a painted crucifixion scene known as Our Lord of Miracles. The original painting is found in the Church of the Nazarenes in downtown Lima. It is a national patrimony and is a living symbol of the authenticity of the folk piety of the Peruvian people.

The Peruvian Church—bishops, priests—accept the Lord of Miracles as part of tradition and integrate its devotions into the Liturgical Year. Its feast day is liturgically observed on October 28. The whole month of October is practically a second Lent, with fasting, penances, hymns, devotions, Masses. Many receive the sacrament of reconciliation during the month of October.

In churches many devotees will pass by the tabernacle where there is reserved the Blessed Sacrament to pray immediately in front of the Lord of Miracles. What is the relation between pictures and statues of Christ, such as the Lord of Miracles, and the Eucharist itself?

In Peru and in many parts of the world there are any number of images and statues of Christ. Almost every region of the countries of Latin America has its own image of Christ and of the Blessed Virgin Mary.

To begin with, an image is just that: it is a painting, a cross, a statue with the face, the body, the figure of Jesus. He who was born of Mary, Jesus of Nazareth, is a human being. And so we hunt for images that we can see, touch, carry in processions, or hang in medals around our necks. He who was crucified was not a phantasm or something purely spiritual such as an invisible angel. The many representations of Jesus remind us that the history of salvation is an authentic part of human history. "We believe in one Lord Jesus Christ. . . . For our sake he was crucified under Pontius Pilate, suffered, died and was buried."

And so what we have is an image, a figure, a representation of Jesus. It is made of wood, of plaster, of leather, of paints, of oils. In this sense a statue or image is not an idol. We honor, we respect the image which is a historical human work. We do not adore the statue. We are not talking about idolatry.

Those in Peru know very well the history of the painting of the Lord of Miracles. This is true of every painting or carving. Each has a distinctive artist, comes from a historical tradition, evokes very special sentiments from its observers, especially where those observers have devotions toward that particular statue of Our Lord.

Yet we adore only God. We adore Jesus, the Son of God, true God. We never adore an image insofar as it is an image. Our faith and our devotion direct us toward that person who is represented by the image.

I am here before Jesus in the Blessed Sacrament. What is the difference between our reactions to the Eucharist and those devotions directed to paintings and statues, such as Our Lord of Miracles?

Of course, what I have here in the Eucharist is bread, a consecrated Host. It is a sacrament, a material thing that through the power of the Holy Spirit makes present the mystery of Christ. The sacraments are not artificial historical presentations as, for example, movies or TV shows about the life of Christ. The sacraments are not theater. The Mass is not a dramatization with Christ seated at a table with the apostles. The Mass is a sacrament where bread and wine, along with distinctive actions, blessings, and remembrances, renew the memorial of that which Jesus did at the Last Supper, on the cross, and in his resurrection.

The rites, actions, and prayers of the sacraments do not use images or representations of Christ. They have power and efficacy because they are symbols. A rite, a symbol speaks to us in a very special way. Our faith understands that a sacramental action realizes an interior, spiritual effect. In the Eucharist, through the consecrated bread, our faith is directed immediately to Christ present; our attitude is an attitude of reverence; or, even better to say, it is an attitude of adoration. "We adore Thee, Oh Christ, and we bless Thee." The Eucharist is not an idol, because we adore the very divinity of Christ present in the consecrated Host.

As we saw, the painting of the Lord of Miracles, like all such paintings and statues, has its own history. It was painted over an adobe wall by a poor black laborer in a slum area of Lima around 1650. It has survived (miraculously) any number of earthquakes in Lima. All the present paintings are copies of this one original painting in the Church of the Nazarenes where a group of cloistered sisters cares for it. All paintings and statues have their distinct histories. Obviously, Our Lady of Guadalupe has its own history.

However, the sacraments direct me immediately to the person of Christ and to the one universal history of salvation. The sacraments as such do not have a distinct style of art.

The sacrament of baptism is the same in all parts of the world: in China, in Africa, in India, or in any of our parishes. The Mass is celebrated in all the languages of the human family and there are different styles of rites, of song, dance, processions, and so on. But the faith and the adoration of the faithful are directed always and immediately to Christ, our Redeemer, who has saved us by his death and resurrection.

Devotions to Our Lord of Miracles and to statues of Christ are very good. The Lord of Miracles is a good example of the way that the Christian faith has been inculturated thoroughly into the history, traditions, and culture of the Peruvian people. It is a manifestation of a profound faith very much alive.

But I dare not allow myself to become confused. Christ is the one and only savior, the same today, yesterday, and always. The celebrations of the sacraments in the Catholic Church are special moments when the mystery of Christ becomes present in my life.

In all cultures, in every moment of history, in all parts of the world, the same Christ is present in the simplicity of the eucharistic bread:

> We adore Thee, Oh Christ, and we bless Thee.
> Who by your cross and resurrection have set us free!

CHAPTER THIRTY

Mary and Martha

The Gospel of Saint Luke says: "Mary . . . sat at the Lord's feet and listened to what he was saying" (Luke 10:39).

There is a tradition in the Church that holds that Mary, the sister of Martha, is the model or example of the contemplative life.

I find myself here at this moment in adoration of the Blessed Sacrament. I am, like Mary, seated at the feet of the Lord to hear his word in the depths of my heart. The attitude and the posture of Mary are of love, of hearing, of contemplation.

"But Martha was distracted by her many tasks" (Luke 10:40).

Unannounced, late in the day, Jesus had arrived at the house of his friends, Mary, Martha, and Lazarus. "Now as they went on their way, he entered a certain village, where a woman named Martha welcomed him into her home" (Luke 10:38). When someone comes late in the day, by the culture of that place, it was the custom to serve a small lunch to a passing visitor or friend. But Martha, overwhelmed by the person who had arrived at the house, began to prepare a big dinner and she needed the help of her sister, Mary. "So she came to him [Jesus] and asked, 'Lord, do you not care that my sister has left me to do all the work by myself? Tell her then to help me'" (Luke 10:40).

Jesus answered her, "Martha, don't make a big deal over it! Let's take a little tea and bread and nothing more. Mary's right. Let's take a light lunch and keep talking."

We all know the situation. A visitor arrives and many times someone must tell the host: "Please, now, just sit down. We came to visit and to talk, not to be served as if we were in a restaurant." "Martha, Martha, you are worried and distracted by many things; there is need of only one thing. Mary has chosen the better part, which will not be taken away from her" (Luke 10:41-42).

It is important to note that in the Gospel of Saint Luke this episode of Martha and Mary comes at the beginning of a series of instructions that Jesus makes about prayer. It is in this same section where one of the disciples asks Jesus: "Lord, teach us to pray" (Luke 11:1), and Jesus taught them the Our Father.

He also speaks of the father of a family who gets up in the middle of the night to give bread to a friend. How much more will the heavenly Father give the Holy Spirit to those who ask him (Luke 11:13). It is clear that to hear the word of Jesus is the beginning of the life of prayer for every believer.

There is no need to make a big distinction between action and prayer. Both are necessary. I know that in the course of every day I have work to do and many activities to attend to. But at the same time, I feel moments when I need silence, reflection, to "sit myself down at the feet of the Lord and to hear his word." These moments before the Blessed Sacrament are privileged moments to hear the Word of the Lord in the depths of my heart.

There is something more in this visit of Jesus to the home of Martha and Mary. Jesus arrived at the house to eat. Friends of Jesus are seated around the table to talk, to dialogue, to share. If it is only a serving of a simple lunch with tea and bread it is a moment of intimacy.

How many times (especially in the Gospel of Luke) we find Jesus seated at a table, eating, sharing, conversing. The Pharisees accuse Jesus of "eating with sinners." Jesus himself takes on the words of his antagonists saying: "The Son of Man has come eating and drinking, and you say, 'Look, a glutton and a drunkard, a friend of tax collectors and sinners!'" (Luke 7:34).

We might say that every time Jesus is eating with people around a table that this is a pre-figuring of the Eucharist. Until the culminating moment when Jesus is seated with his disciples to celebrate together the paschal meal, the Last Supper, the first Eucharist.

After the resurrection Jesus appeared to his disciples several times in the context of eating. The two disciples walking to Emmaus explained to the rest: "They told what had happened on the road, and how he had been made known to them in the breaking of the bread" (Luke 24:35).

And when Jesus himself appeared to the whole group, showing them his pierced hands and feet, he said: "Have you anything here to eat?" (Luke 24:41). In the Gospel of Saint John, the resurrected Jesus says: "'Come, and have breakfast.' . . . Jesus came and took the bread and gave it to them, and did the same with the fish" (John 21:12-13).

We, too, recognize Jesus in the sharing of bread. I recognize Jesus in the eucharistic bread. This is the living bread come down from heaven. This is the bread offered as gifts during the offertory of the Mass, fruit of the earth and work of human hands. Sometimes we forget all the human labor that goes into the bread we share at Mass. There are many workers, such as Martha, who help us so that we have bread.

There are those many moments when all the Marthas of the world—and also myself—are worried and distracted about our daily tasks. Yet we should take time to sit down at the feet of Jesus to hear his word.

So now it is my turn. Jesus has invited me here. I can sit down at the feet of my Lord.

Let me hear his word in my heart.

CHAPTER THIRTY-ONE

Mary and the Eucharist

Many of the prayers and devotions offered before the Blessed Sacrament are prayers, songs, the recitation of the rosary in honor of Mary the Mother of Jesus. It seems that many people pray to Mary because they do not have other resources to pass the time during a Holy Hour. The rosary and traditional hymns to Mary are well known and they create a good setting for community prayers. All this is very good.

In the Sermon on the Mount Jesus said: "When you are praying, do not heap up empty phrases as the Gentiles do; for they think that they will be heard because of their many words" (Matt 6:7).

Isn't it true that in the recitation of the rosary we multiply many words? Well, yes and no. Of course, it is evident that in the praying of the rosary there is a torrent of words, the repetition of Our Fathers and Hail Marys.

For me it is the honest truth that at times I pray the rosary as a pure routine. The beads slip through my fingers, the words pass over my lips, but my thoughts are for the birds. This is my fault and it is not the fault of the rosary as a style of prayer. In fact, at every moment of the recitation of the rosary I should reflect on one of the fifteen mysteries, each of which focuses upon a very distinct moment in the history of salvation, mostly in the life of Jesus and in the glories of Mary.

Yet praying the rosary is *not* the simple multiplication of words that Jesus criticizes. When I pray the rosary before the Blessed Sacrament I can meditate on the annunciation of the Angel to Mary, the visitation of Mary to Elizabeth, the birth of the Savior, the presentation of Jesus in the Temple, the finding of Jesus in the Temple.

That is to say, along with the Virgin Mary, the Mother of Jesus, my attention is directed to Jesus himself.

At the same time, the repetition of well-known words helps to free my mind and open my heart immediately to the presence of Jesus. There is a traditional practice very common in many religions called the mantra. A mantra is a type of chant or short phrase. By a simple, disciplined repeating of a few words I can free myself from other thoughts or distractions and in some manner I can free myself and feel myself to be in the presence of God.

The prayers and dynamics of the charismatics have something very similar to this. The repetition of some chants or a few phrases can elevate one into a type of trance. At times this can go to extremes and create a kind of fanaticism. But with caution and balance such prayers can be quite positive.

But in any case, the recitation of the rosary is much more than a simple mantra. To pray the rosary is always a meditation on the mysteries of the lives of Jesus and Mary.

The words of the Hail Mary are words taken directly from the New Testament. The Hail Mary is a biblical prayer, almost like one of the psalms. "Hail Mary, full of grace, the Lord is with you"—these are the words of the greeting of the archangel Gabriel to Mary at the moment of the annunciation. The new English translation is: "Greetings, favored one! The Lord is with you" (Luke 1:28).

"Blessed are you among women, and blessed is the fruit of your womb" is also taken from the New Testament. These are the words of Elizabeth to Mary at the moment of the Visitation. The new translation retains these exact words (Luke 1:42).

Finally, in the second part of the Hail Mary we beg Mary, the Mother of Jesus, to pray for us sinners, now, and at the hour of our death. These are honest, authentic, sincere prayers at any time and at all times.

The bottom line in the praying of the rosary is the mystery of the incarnation. The Word of God took on our flesh. Mary conceived of the Holy Spirit. "Therefore, the child to be born will be holy; he will be called Son of God" (Luke 1:35). Mary answered: "Here I am, the servant of the Lord; let it be with me according to your word" (Luke 1:38). In the countryside outside of Bethlehem "she gave birth to her firstborn son and wrapped him in bands of cloth, and laid him in a manger" (Luke 2:7).

Devotion to Mary is within the mystery of our salvation by Jesus.

> Meanwhile, standing near the cross of Jesus [was] his mother. . . . When Jesus saw his mother and the disciple whom he loved standing beside her, he said to his mother, "Woman, here is your son." Then he said to the disciple, "Here is your mother." And from that hour the disciple took her into his own home (John 19:25-27).

From that hour until now, here, in the presence of Jesus in the Blessed Sacrament, I have as my mother Mary, the Mother of Jesus, the Mother of the Church.

My devotions to Mary will never allow me to forget that her Son is the only Savior, today, yesterday, and forever, because Mary always brings me to Jesus.

Mary says to me what she said to the servants at the wedding of Cana. "Do whatever he tells you" (John 2:5).

In the mystery of the Assumption I believe that Mary, body and soul, is with the resurrected Christ in the glory of heaven.

It is this same Christ, glorified and resurrected, who has remained with me in the eucharistic bread. O Mary, help me to deepen my faith!

CHAPTER THIRTY-TWO

The Eucharist and Prayers of Petition

I am before Christ in the Blessed Sacrament, seated at the feet of the Lord. I open my heart to sentiments of love, intimacy, and thanksgiving.

Contemplation is the attitude of silence, of hearing, of paying attention—in this case—to the love of God present in Christ in the sacrament.

But, like everyone else, I have my necessities, my petitions, my special prayers before the Lord. For many people the only prayer they know is the prayer of asking: "O God, I am in bad health! For my Aunt! That my children find work! That there be harmony in our family! For peace in the world!" There is no stopping this list of prayers.

It would seem that eucharistic contemplation does not permit prayers of petition. Let us study this point with care.

It is evident that in all parts of the Sacred Scriptures there are many prayers of supplication, of pleading, of petition to God. Yet Jesus said on the Sermon on the Mount: "When you are praying, do not heap up empty phrases as the Gentiles do; for they think that they will be heard because of their many words. Do not be like them, for your Father knows what you need before you ask him" (Matt 6:7-8).

In the conversation of Jesus with his disciples at the Last Supper in the Gospel of John, Jesus says: "Very truly, I tell you, if you ask anything of the Father in my name, he will give it to you. Until now you have not asked for anything in my name. Ask and you will receive, so that your joy may be complete" (John 16:23-24).

Here we have the first condition for a prayer of petition to God: the attitude of faith and confidence; the confidence of a child before a loving father; the faith that asks of God the Father in the name of his Son, Jesus. What a simple but very profound lesson we have from Jesus.

In Saint Luke we read:

> For everyone who asks receives, and everyone who searches finds, and for everyone who knocks, the door will be opened. Is there anyone among you who, if your child asks for a fish, will give a snake instead of a fish? Or if the child asks for an egg, will give a scorpion? If you then, who are evil, know how to give good gifts to your children, how much more will the heavenly Father give the Holy Spirit to those who ask him! (Luke 11:10-13).

One can find the same message in Matthew 7:7-12.

The Gospel of Saint Luke gives various examples of "the need to pray always and not to lose heart" (Luke 18:1). There is the case of a widow who constantly bothers the unjust judge who had "no fear of God and no respect for anyone, yet because this widow keeps bothering me, I will grant her justice" (Luke 18:4-5). "And will not God grant justice to his chosen ones who cry to him day and night?" (Luke 18:7).

Many of the psalms are prayers of petition to God. So many of them begin with the invocation to God. "Hear a just cause, O LORD; attend to my cry" (Ps 17:1). There then follows a description of a very precise historical setting of the psalmist and his community. There are prayers, motives, reasons, descriptions. Jesus taught his disciples his own prayer: the Our Father. For all time there is no better prayer than the Lord's Prayer.

My theme today before the Blessed Sacrament is eucharistic contemplation and the prayers of petition. I should hear some words of Saint Paul to the Romans.

> Likewise the Spirit helps us in our weakness; for we do not know how to pray as we ought, but that very Spirit intercedes with sighs too deep for words. And God, who searches the heart, knows what is the mind of the Spirit, because the Spirit intercedes for the saints according to the will of God (Rom 8:26-27).

And so I ask myself: How can I approach Christ in the sacrament of the Eucharist with an attitude of faith and confidence in the same sentiments of which Saint Paul writes?

The prayer of Jesus in Gethsemane was: "My Father, if it is possible, let this cup pass from me; yet not what I want but what you want" (Matt 26:39).

Of course, I have my worries, my needs, my uncertainties; I have my fears, things that disturb me, things that molest me. That is how all of us are and that is how I present myself before the Lord. "Here I am, Lord, a sinner, with many, many needs."

However, before my Lord, I do not have to multiply words, looking only at myself and at my problems. I ought to open my heart to Jesus crucified and risen in the Sacred Host. "Lord, have mercy on me, a sinner."

"Pray to your Father who is in secret; and your Father who sees in secret will reward you" (Matt 6:6).